BLOND'S CIVIL PROCEDURE

Yeazell Edition

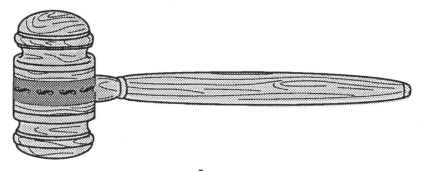

by
Neil C. Blond

Yeazel Edition Revised
by Mark Monack
Robert M. Novick

S&G SULZBURGER & GRAHAM
PUBLISHING, Ltd.
NEW YORK

(800) 366-7086

ALSO AVAILABLE IN THIS SERIES:

Blond's Administrative Law
Blond's Civil Procedure
Blond's Constitutional Law
Blond's Contracts
Blond's Corporate Tax
Blond's Corporations
Blond's Criminal Law
Blond's Criminal Procedure
Blond's Essay Questions — Contracts
Blond's Essay Questions — Torts
Blond's Evidence
Blond's Family Law
Blond's Income Tax
Blond's International Law
Blond's Multistate Questions
Blond's Professional Responsibility Questions
Blond's Property
Blond's Torts

How To Use This Book

"You teach yourself the law, we teach you how to think"
- Professor Kingsfield, The Paper Chase

Law school is very different from your previous educational experiences. In the past, course material was presented in a straightforward manner both in lectures and texts. You did well by memorizing and regurgitating. In law school, your fat casebooks are stuffed with material, most of which will be useless when finals arrive. Your professors ask a lot of questions but don't seem to be teaching you either the law or how to think. Sifting through voluminous material seeking out the important concepts is a hard, time-consuming chore. We've done that job for you. This book will help you study effectively. We hope to teach you the law and how to think.

Preparing for class

Most students start their first year by reading and briefing all their cases. They spend too much time copying unimportant details. After finals they realize they wasted time on facts that were useless on the exam.

Case Clips

Case Clips help you focus on what your professor wants you to get out of your cases. Facts, Issues, and Rules are carefully and succinctly stated. Left out are details irrelevant to what you need to learn from the case. In general, we skip procedural matters in lower courts. We don't care which party is the appellant or petitioner because the trivia is not relevant to the law. Case Clips should be read before you read the actual case. You will have a good idea what to look for in the case, and appreciate the significance of what you are reading. Inevitably you will not have time to read all your cases before class. Case Clips allow you to prepare for class in about five minutes. You will be able to follow the discussion and listen without fear of being called upon.

This book contains a case clip of every major case covered in your casebook. Each case clip is followed by a code identifying the casebook(s) in which it appears as a principal case. Since we accommodate all the major casebooks, the case clips may not follow the same sequence as they do in your text. The easiest way to study is to leaf through your text and find the corresponding case in this book by checking the table of cases.

"Should I read all the cases even if they aren't from my casebook?"

Yes, if you feel you have the time. Most major cases from other texts will be covered at least as a note case in your book. The principles of these cases are universal and the fact patterns should help your understanding. The Case Clips are written in a way that should provide a tremendous amount of understanding in a relatively short period of time.

Hanau Charts

When asked how he managed to graduate in the top ten percent of his class at one of the ten most prestigious law schools in the land, Paul Hanau introduced his system of flow charts now known as Hanau Charts.

A very common complaint among first year students is that they "can't put it all together." When you are reading 400 pages a week it is difficult to remember how the last case relates to the first and how November's readings relate to September's. It's hard to understand the relationship between different torts topics when you have read cases for three or four other classes in between. Hanau Charts will help you put the whole course together. They are designed to help you memorize fundamentals. They reinforce your learning by showing you the material from another perspective.

Outlines

More than one hundred lawyers and law students were interviewed as part of the development of this series. Most complained that their casebooks did not teach them the law and were far too voluminous to be useful before an exam. They also told us that the commercial outlines they purchased were excellent when used as hornbooks to explain the law, but were too wordy and redundant to be effective during the weeks before finals. Few students can read four 500-page outlines during the last month of classes. It is virtually impossible to memorize that much material and even harder to decide what is important. Almost every student interviewed said he or she studied from homemade outlines. We've written the outline you should use to study.

"But writing my own outline will be a learning experience."

True, but unfortunately many students spend so much time outlining they don't leave time to learn and memorize. Many students told us they spent six weeks outlining, and only one day studying before each final!

Mnemonics

Most law students spend too much time reading, and not enough time memorizing. Mnemonics are included to help you organize your essays and spot issues. They highlight what is important and which areas deserve your time.

TABLE OF CONTENTS

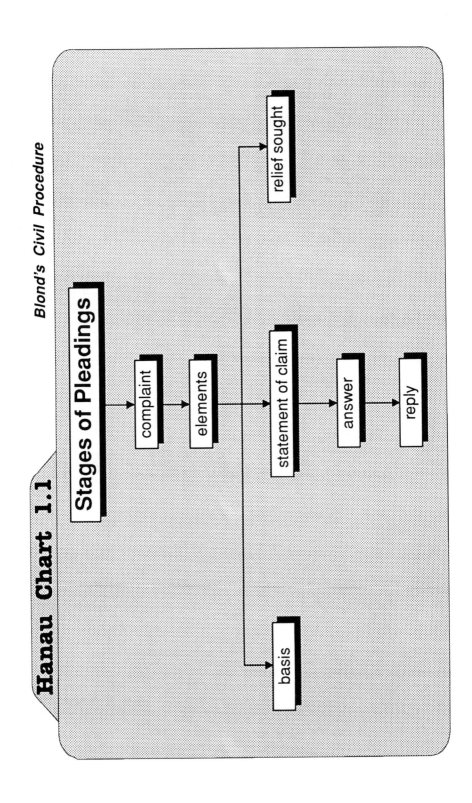

Hanau Chart 1.1

Stages of Pleadings

complaint → elements → statement of claim → answer → reply

relief sought

basis

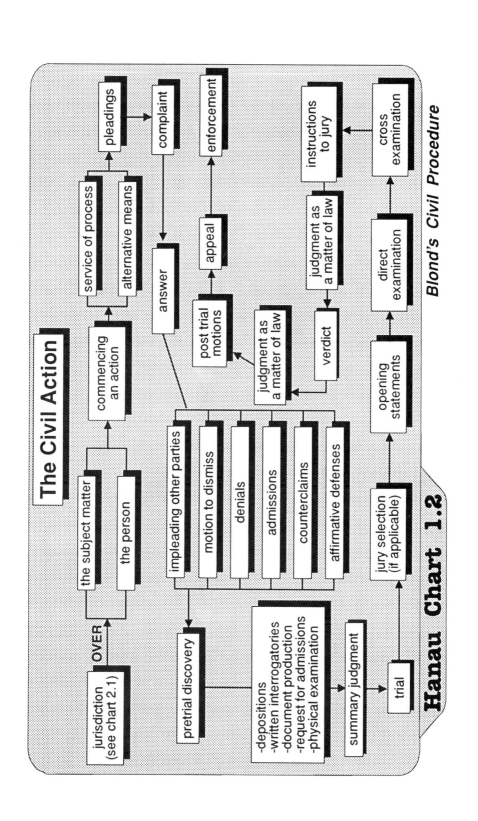

The Civil Action

Blond's Civil Procedure

Hanau Chart 1.2

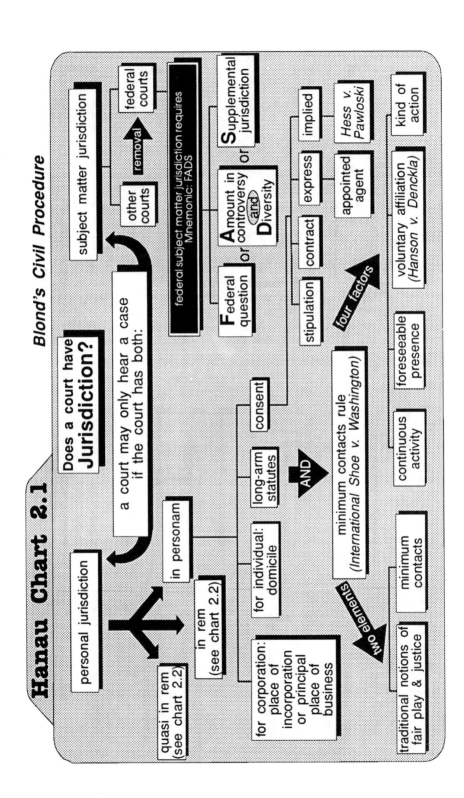

Hanau Chart 2.1

Blond's Civil Procedure

Does a court have Jurisdiction?

a court may only hear a case if the court has both:

subject matter jurisdiction
- other courts
- federal courts
  - removal

federal subject matter jurisdiction requires Mnemonic: FADS
- **F**ederal question or
- **A**mount in controversy **and D**iversity or
- **S**upplemental jurisdiction

personal jurisdiction
- quasi in rem (see chart 2.2)
- in rem (see chart 2.2)
- in personam
  - for individual: domicile
  - for corporation: place of incorporation or principal place of business
  - long-arm statutes
  - consent

AND

minimum contacts rule (International Shoe v. Washington)

two elements
- minimum contacts
- traditional notions of fair play & justice

four factors
- stipulation
- contract
- express
- implied
  - appointed agent
  - Hess v. Pawloski
- foreseeable presence
- continuous activity
- voluntary affiliation (Hanson v. Denckla)
- kind of action

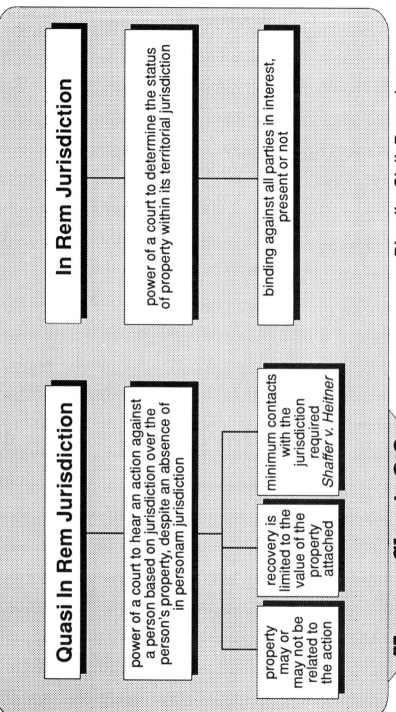

Quasi In Rem Jurisdiction

power of a court to hear an action against a person based on jurisdiction over the person's property, despite an absence of in personam jurisdiction

property may or may not be related to the action

recovery is limited to the value of the property attached

minimum contacts with the jurisdiction required *Shaffer v. Heitner*

In Rem Jurisdiction

power of a court to determine the status of property within its territorial jurisdiction

binding against all parties in interest, present or not

Hanau Chart 2.2

Blond's Civil Procedure

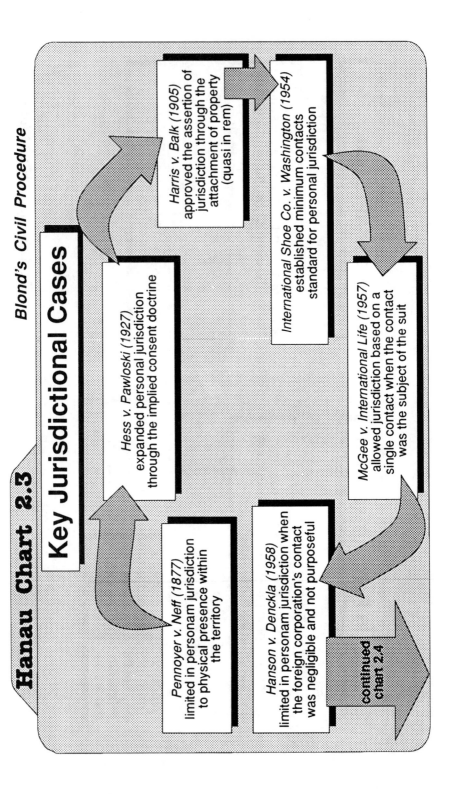

Blond's Civil Procedure

Hanau Chart 2.3

Key Jurisdictional Cases

Pennoyer v. Neff (1877) limited in personam jurisdiction to physical presence within the territory

Hess v. Pawloski (1927) expanded personal jurisdiction through the implied consent doctrine

Harris v. Balk (1905) approved the assertion of jurisdiction through the attachment of property (quasi in rem)

International Shoe Co. v. Washington (1954) established minimum contacts standard for personal jurisdiction

Hanson v. Denckla (1958) limited in personam jurisdiction when the foreign corporation's contact was negligible and not purposeful

McGee v. International Life (1957) allowed jurisdiction based on a single contact when the contact was the subject of the suit

continued chart 2.4

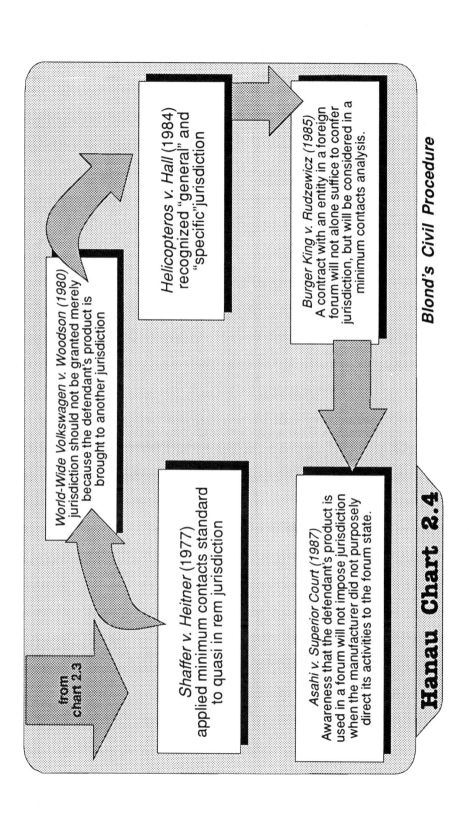

World-Wide Volkswagen v. Woodson (1980) jurisdiction should not be granted merely because the defendant's product is brought to another jurisdiction

Helicopteros v. Hall (1984) recognized "general" and "specific" jurisdiction

Burger King v. Rudzewicz (1985) A contract with an entity in a foreign forum will not alone suffice to confer jurisdiction, but will be considered in a minimum contacts analysis.

from chart 2.3

Shaffer v. Heitner (1977) applied minimum contacts standard to quasi in rem jurisdiction

Asahi v. Superior Court (1987) Awareness that the defendant's product is used in a forum will not impose jurisdiction when the manufacturer did not purposely direct its activities to the forum state.

Blond's Civil Procedure

Hanau Chart 2.4

Hanau Chart 2.5

Blond's Civil Procedure

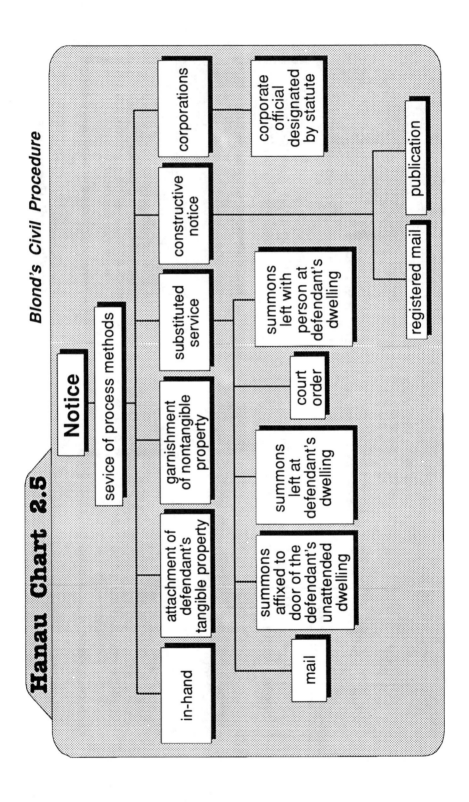

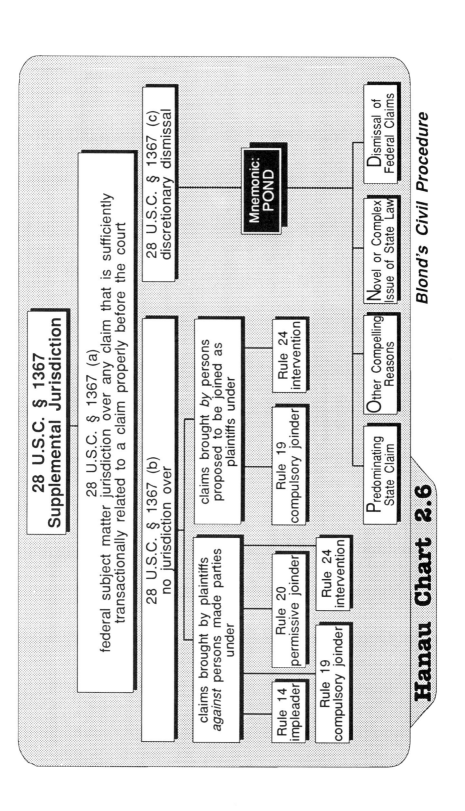

**28 U.S.C. § 1367
Supplemental Jurisdiction**

28 U.S.C. § 1367 (a)
federal subject matter jurisdiction over any claim that is sufficiently transactionally related to a claim properly before the court

28 U.S.C. § 1367 (c)
discretionary dismissal

Mnemonic:
POND

28 U.S.C. § 1367 (b)
no jurisdiction over

claims brought by plaintiffs *against* persons made parties under

Rule 14
impleader

Rule 20
permissive joinder

Rule 19
compulsory joinder

Rule 24
intervention

claims brought *by* persons proposed to be joined as plaintiffs under

Rule 19
compulsory joinder

Rule 24
intervention

Predominating State Claim

Other Compelling Reasons

Novel or Complex Issue of State Law

Dismissal of Federal Claims

Hanau Chart 2.6

Blond's Civil Procedure

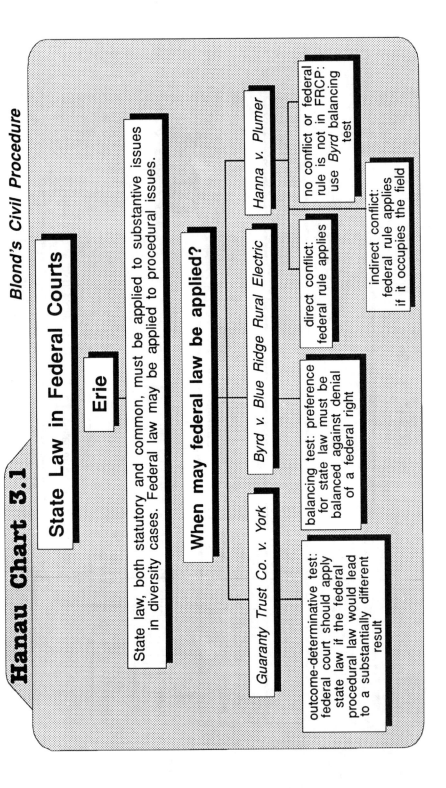

Hanau Chart 3.1

Blond's Civil Procedure

State Law in Federal Courts

Erie

State law, both statutory and common, must be applied to substantive issues in diversity cases. Federal law may be applied to procedural issues.

When may federal law be applied?

Guaranty Trust Co. v. York

outcome-determinative test: federal court should apply state law if the federal procedural law would lead to a substantially different result

Byrd v. Blue Ridge Rural Electric

balancing test: preference for state law must be balanced against denial of a federal right

direct conflict: federal rule applies

Hanna v. Plumer

no conflict or federal rule is not in FRCP: use *Byrd* balancing test

indirect conflict: federal rule applies if it occupies the field

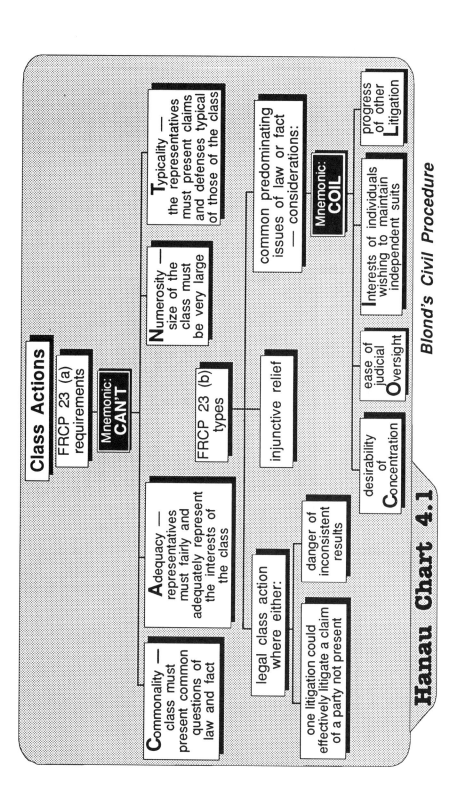

Class Actions

FRCP 23 (a) requirements

Mnemonic: **CAN'T**

Commonality — class must present common questions of law and fact

Adequacy — representatives must fairly and adequately represent the interests of the class

Numerosity — size of the class must be very large

Typicality — the representatives must present claims and defenses typical of those of the class

FRCP 23 (b) types

legal class action where either:

one litigation could effectively litigate a claim of a party not present

danger of inconsistent results

injunctive relief

common predominating issues of law or fact — considerations:

Mnemonic: **COIL**

desirability of **C**oncentration

ease of judicial **O**versight

Interests of individuals wishing to maintain independent suits

progress of other **L**itigation

Blond's Civil Procedure

Hanau Chart 4.1

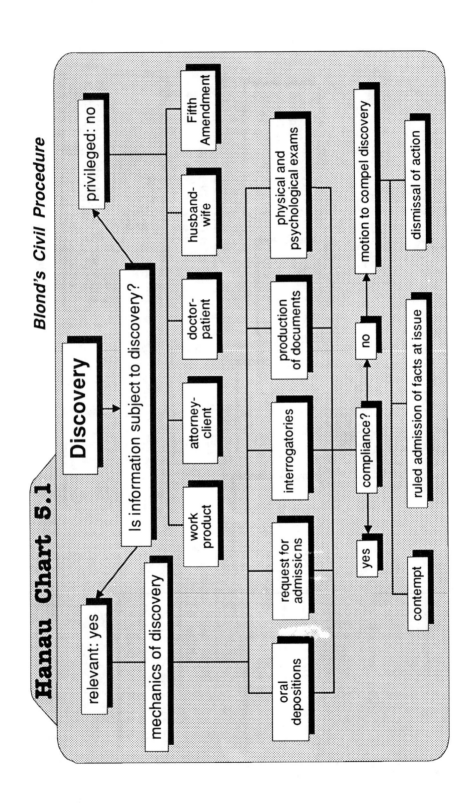

Hanau Chart 5.1

Blond's Civil Procedure

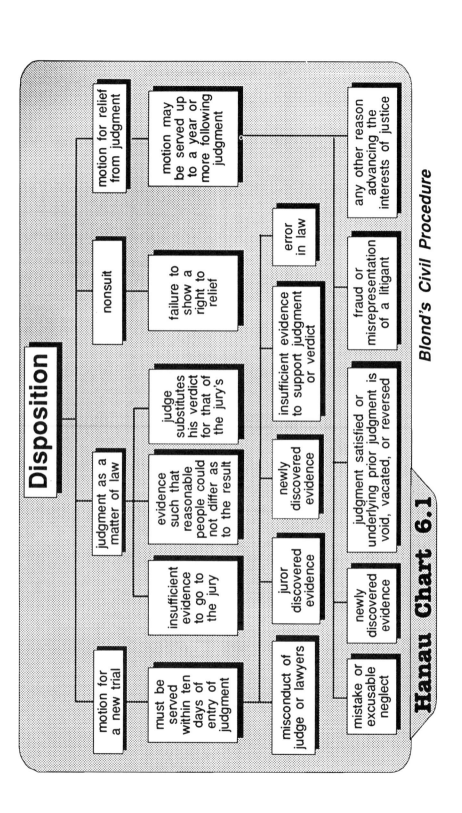

Disposition

motion for relief from judgment
- motion may be served up to a year or more following judgment
  - any other reason advancing the interests of justice
  - fraud or misrepresentation of a litigant
  - judgment satisfied or underlying prior judgment is void, vacated, or reversed
  - newly discovered evidence
  - mistake or excusable neglect

nonsuit
- failure to show a right to relief
  - error in law
  - insufficient evidence to support judgment or verdict

judgment as a matter of law
- judge substitutes his verdict for that of the jury's
- evidence such that reasonable people could not differ as to the result
- insufficient evidence to go to the jury

motion for a new trial
- must be served within ten days of entry of judgment
  - newly discovered evidence
  - juror discovered evidence
  - misconduct of judge or lawyers

Blond's Civil Procedure

Hanau Chart 6.1

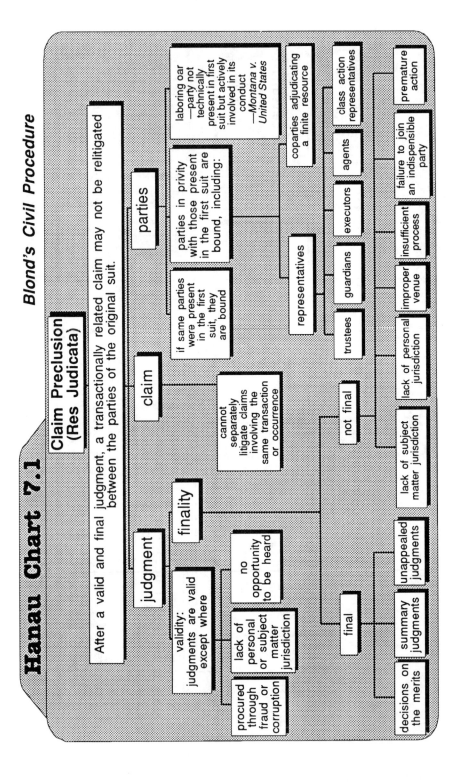

Hanau Chart 7.1

Blond's Civil Procedure

Claim Preclusion (Res Judicata)

After a valid and final judgment, a transactionally related claim may not be relitigated between the parties of the original suit.

judgment

validity: judgments are valid except where
- procured through fraud or corruption
- lack of personal or subject matter jurisdiction
- no opportunity to be heard

finality
- final
  - decisions on the merits
  - summary judgments
  - unappealed judgments
- not final
  - lack of subject matter jurisdiction
  - lack of personal jurisdiction
  - improper venue
  - insufficient process
  - failure to join an indispensible party
  - premature action

claim

cannot separately litigate claims involving the same transaction or occurrence

parties

if same parties were present in the first suit, they are bound

parties in privity with those present in the first suit are bound, including:
- laboring oar —party not technically present in first suit but actively involved in its conduct —*Montana v. United States*
- coparties adjudicating a finite resource
- representatives
  - trustees
  - guardians
  - executors
  - agents
  - class action representatives

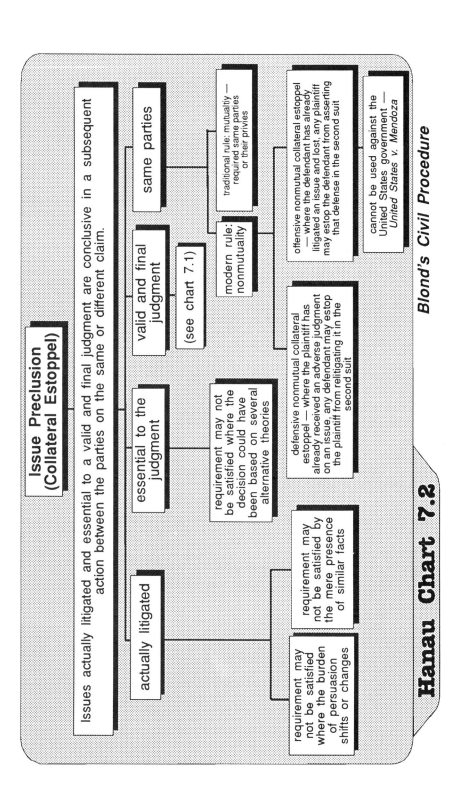

Issue Preclusion (Collateral Estoppel)

Issues actually litigated and essential to a valid and final judgment are conclusive in a subsequent action between the parties on the same or different claim.

actually litigated

requirement may not be satisfied by the mere presence of similar facts

requirement may not be satisfied where the burden of persuasion shifts or changes

essential to the judgment

requirement may not be satisfied where the decision could have been based on several alternative theories

defensive nonmutual collateral estoppel — where the plaintiff has already received an adverse judgment on an issue, any defendant may estop the plaintiff from relitigating it in the second suit

valid and final judgment

(see chart 7.1)

same parties

traditional rule: mutuality — required same parties or their privies

modern rule: nonmutuality

offensive nonmutual collateral estoppel — where the defendant has already litigated an issue and lost, any plaintiff may estop the defendant from asserting that defense in the second suit

cannot be used against the United States government — *United States v. Mendoza*

Hanau Chart 7.2

Blond's Civil Procedure

Chapter 1

INTRODUCTION

As an introduction to civil procedure, it is sometimes helpful to look at the process of a civil action, both the procedures and issues involved.

I. COMMENCING THE ACTION

The plaintiff must notify the defendant of the suit being brought, what court is asserting jurisdiction over the case, and something of the nature of the case (although exactly what is needed is unclear and will be discussed in greater detail elsewhere in the book).

There are various methods of commencing the action, but the most common is service of process.

II. PLEADINGS

A. Filing the Complaint
The plaintiff must also notify the court of the impending case. This is done by filing a complaint.

1. Benefits of Being a Plaintiff
As plaintiff, a party has great leeway in framing the structure of the case:

a. The plaintiff gets to choose (at least initially) whether federal or state courts will be used.

b. The plaintiff chooses (also initially) the state or district in which the suit is brought.

c. The plaintiff initially defines the issues involved, including what parties to join as defendants, what relief to seek (injunctive, monetary or both), and how much.

2. Burdens of Being a Plaintiff

   a. To the Court
   The plaintiff must also carefully frame the nature of the case, for if the plaintiff fails to set forth certain very specific requirements (which will be discussed in detail in Chapter 2), the case may be dismissed.

   b. To the Defendant
   The plaintiff must also set forth in the complaint enough information such that the defendant may identify and respond to the allegations.

B. Responsive Pleadings
What follows from the initial pleadings are a series of responses by both parties.

1. Purpose
The pleadings are designed to identify the precise issues disputed by the parties, thereby saving both the courts and parties time and money that might have been wasted arguing irrelevant or undisputed issues. However, pleadings may also be used to harass parties or delay the action.

2. Content
In the pleadings, a party may:

   a. Amend the Complaint

   b. Assert an Affirmative Defense

   c. Assert a Counterclaim

   d. Implead a Third Party

   e. Make a Motion to Dismiss

   f. Admit and Deny Factual Allegations

III. DISCOVERY

After the pleadings, parties use various pretrial procedures in order to unearth knowledge in the other party's possession, or in the possession of witnesses. Discovery, however, is not designed to allow a party to discover their opponent's legal strategy, and there are several safeguards and sanctions available to courts and parties to ensure proper discovery. Some discovery tools available to the litigator are:

A. Depositions
Used to orally interview witnesses.

B. Written Interrogatories
Used to compel written answers to submitted questionnaires.

C. Subpoenas Duces Tecum
Used to compel production of documents.

D. Medical Examinations
Either physical or psychological, they must be for a specific and necessary purpose, such as determining the extent of injuries, or determining mental capacity.

IV. TRIAL

A. Jury Trials

1. Trial by jury is a right in certain actions (criminal trial, most federal court suits).

2. Jurors are usually selected by the judge.

3. Peremptory challenges to jury selection are allowed.

B. Trial Procedure

1. Order of Parties
The plaintiff always goes first.

2. Opening Statements

The parties briefly explain their positions and what they hope to prove.

3. Questioning Witnesses

   a. Direct Examination
      Witness' initial questioning. Evidence may be introduced through a witness' reference to it. The evidence must comply with the appropriate rules of evidence (state law or the Federal Rules of Evidence).

   b. Cross-Examination
      Witness' answers to direct examination may be probed, or additional information known to the witness may be brought out.

   c. Redirect
      After cross-examination the party who called the witness may question him about matters brought out in cross-examination.

4. Motion for Summary Judgment
   If a party has not produced enough evidence to sustain its claim, and the judge feels that no reasonable jury could find otherwise, the judge may summarily dismiss the claim or issue of law involved or, alternatively, direct the jury that the issue involved cannot be decided otherwise.

5. Closing Arguments
   Parties summarize their version of the case.

6. Jury Instruction
   Judge tells jury the relevant law, and instructs them as to the relevant burdens of persuasion, as well as any presumptions they may be entitled to make. If there is to be a general verdict with interrogatories or a special verdict, the judge will also instruct the jury on these issues.

7. Verdict

   a. General Verdict
      Jury decides which party prevails.

b. General Verdict With Interrogatories
In complicated cases, a judge may require a jury to answer a questionnaire in order to ensure that the jury fully understood the issues involved.

c. Special Verdict
The jury only decides limited factual issues that the judge uses to reach a final decision.

V.   APPEAL

A.   Reversing the Jury
A jury may only be overturned where no evidence submitted could have resulted in a jury deciding as it did.

B.   Reversing the Judge

1. Factual Findings
A judge's findings of fact may be reversed only where "clearly erroneous." This standard is supposed to be very high.

2. Procedural Findings
A case may be successfully appealed where a judge's procedural conclusions constitute an "abuse of discretion."

3. Legal Findings
Generally, courts will reverse a trial judge who has misapplied the applicable law.

CASE CLIPS

Gordon v. Steele (1974)

Facts: Gordon left her parents home in Pennsylvania to attend college in Idaho. She had an apartment in Idaho and intended to remain there indefinitely, although she returned to Pennsylvania during vacations and maintained a Pennsylvania Driver's License. At age 19, Gordon brought a malpractice action in federal court against two doctors who were Pennsylvania citizens. The defendants moved to dismiss for lack of diversity.

Issue: Where are students who attend out-of-state colleges domiciled?

Rule: In light of the modern trend to treat 18-year-olds as emancipated, a factfinder should determine whether a student has established a new domicile by looking to such circumstances as declarations of intent, exercise of political rights, payment of personal taxes, house of residence, and place of business. In this case, the court found that Gordon was domiciled in Idaho, primarily because she rented an apartment there and had no intent to return to Pennsylvania.

Smith v. Egger (1985)

Facts: Smith filed an action requesting damages and seeking a restraining order against IRS officials who had attempted to levy on Smith's property for past due taxes. The defendants requested reimbursement for their attorneys' fees on grounds that the action was frivolous and without any merit because, inter alia, the claim was barred by statute.

Issue: May defendants recover attorneys' fees expended to defend against frivolous claims?

Rule: Under FRCP 11, parties and/or their attorneys can be held liable for reasonable expenses incurred in defending against signed papers (i.e., pleadings, motions, etc.) that are clearly not grounded in fact, warranted by existing law, or a good faith argument for extension of the law. Here, the plaintiff's original claim was clearly without merit because it was barred by a statute, such that it appeared that the complaints were filed solely to harass and delay tax collection. Therefore, they were liable for the attorneys' fees reasonably incurred in defending against the claims.

Bell v. Novick Transfer Co. (1955)

Facts: In a negligence action arising out of an auto accident, the defendants moved to dismiss on the basis that the complaint did not allege specific acts of negligence, but only that "an accident occurred due to the negligence of the defendants as a result of which the plaintiffs were injured."

Issue: What information must a complaint contain?

Rule: Under FRCP 8, a complaint need only contain a short and plain statement of the claim showing that the pleader is entitled to relief. The defendant may obtain more detailed information later through discovery procedures (e.g., interrogatories, depositions, etc.). Thus, the court held that Bell's complaint was sufficient and overruled Novick Transfer's motion to dismiss.

Note: This action was originally filed in Maryland State court and removed to federal court. Had the action remained in State court, Maryland rules of procedure would have applied under which the complaint may not have been sufficient.

Temple v. Synthes Corp. (1990)

Facts: Temple underwent surgery to have a plate-and-screw device implanted in his spine. After surgery, the screws broke. Synthes manufactured the device. Temple filed a federal suit against Synthes and a separate state action against the doctor and hospital. Synthes filed a motion to dismiss Temple's federal suit for failure to join necessary parties (the doctor and the hospital) pursuant to FRCP 19.

Issue: Are joint tortfeasors indispensable parties under FRCP 19?

Rule: Although there is a public interest in avoiding multiple lawsuits, it is not necessary for all joint tortfeasors to be named as defendants in a single lawsuit. Therefore, joint tortfeasors are not indispensable parties under FRCP 19 and failure to join them is not grounds for dismissal.

Goldinger v. Boron (1973)

Facts: As part of a contract action, Goldinger alleged that the defendant's commission manager agreements were unconscionable. Goldinger filed a Motion to Compel [FRCP 37(a)] Boron to answer an interrogatory that asked whether Boron had entered into new agreements with commission managers and, if so, why changes were made to the agreements.

Issue 1: Can parties obtain discovery of information concerning acts and events that transpired after the cause of action arose?

Rule 1: Discovery of acts and events occurring after the cause of action arose is permitted where there is a possibility that the information sought may be relevant to the subject matter of the pending action, even if that information may not be admissible at trial.

Issue 2:   Does attorney-client privilege protect information from discovery?

Rule 2:   Information is protected from discovery by attorney-client privilege if it satisfies the four-part privilege test: 1) confidence that the communication will not be disclosed, 2) confidentiality of the disclosure, 3) an existing legal relationship between the parties, and 4) if the injury disclosure would cause to the client is greater than the benefit to the factfinder. Under this rule, Baron Oil's agreements are discoverable because they must be read and signed by someone other than the defendant and its attorney (i.e., they are not confidential). The rationale for any changes in the agreements, however, is privileged legal planning and is therefore not discoverable.

Houchins v. American Home Assurance Co. (1991)

Facts: Mr. Houchins was missing for over seven years and, by law, presumed dead. He had two life insurance policies, both of which required that the insured's death be accidental to be entitled to coverage. Mrs. Houchins sued for payment on the policies. American Home moved for summary judgment on the ground that Mrs. Houchins offered no evidence to establish that the death was accidental.

Issue: May a party defeat a motion for summary judgment by offering an inference as evidence of a material fact?

Rule: FRCP 56(c) provides that summary judgment must be granted against a party that fails to make a showing sufficient to establish the existence of an element essential to that party's case. A presumption of a material fact, such as a legal presumption of death, is sufficient to defeat a summary judgment motion. However, an inference based on another inference (e.g., presuming death and then inferring that it was accidental) is too meager to provide evidence sufficient to defeat a summary judgment motion.

Norton v. Snapper Power Equipment (1987)

Facts: Norton was injured when the Snapper mower he was riding slid into a creek; the blade sliced off four of his fingers. The mower was found to be defective because it did not have a "dead man" device to stop the blade. Norton did not know exactly how or when his hand got caught in the blade. After the jury rendered a verdict in favor of Norton, Snapper requested a directed verdict on the grounds that there was not sufficient evidence from which a jury could have found that a "dead-man" device would have reduced or prevented Norton's injuries.

Issue: What is the standard for granting a judgment notwithstanding the verdict?

Rule: A verdict cannot be based on speculation and conjecture. However, a jury can reach a verdict by reconstructing events by drawing inference upon inference. A court should grant judgment notwithstanding the verdict only where the evidence, when viewed in the light most favorable to the nonmoving party, so strongly points in favor of the moving party that reasonable people could not find otherwise.

Rush v. City of Maple Heights (1958)

Facts: Rush was injured when she fell in an accident. She successfully sued for damages to personal property. Then she commenced a new action to recover for her personal injuries.

Issue: When can a plaintiff split a cause of action arising from a single act?

Rule: A plaintiff may maintain only one action arising from a single transaction or occurrence.

Dunn v. Phoenix Newspapers (1984)

Facts: Newspaper home-delivery carriers brought an anti-trust suit against the publisher of two newspapers, alleging illegal price fixing. At a bench trial (i.e., no jury), the court decided in favor of the defendants. The plaintiffs appealed.

Issue: What is the standard for appellate review of a lower court decision?

Rule: On appeal, an appellate court reviews findings of law *de novo* (considers the issues anew). Findings of fact, however, must stand unless the findings are clearly erroneous.

Chapter 2

JURISDICTION

I. OVERVIEW

A court may only hear a case if it has both subject matter jurisdiction and personal jurisdiction:

A. Subject Matter Jurisdiction
Power to adjudicate the kind of case presented.

1. Power to act.

2. The defendant must be provided with adequate notice and opportunity to be heard.

B. Personal Jurisdiction
Power over the parties or property involved.

1. In personam jurisdiction
The court has jurisdiction due to its power over the defendant himself.

2. In rem jurisdiction
The court has jurisdiction due to its power over the property in question.

3. Quasi in rem jurisdiction
The court has jurisdiction by seizing property that belongs to the defendant but is not the property that is the subject of the litigation.

II. SUBJECT MATTER JURISDICTION

A. Defined
Power of a court to decide the kind of action before it.

Mnemonic: **FADES**

B. Federal Question Cases

1. Federal courts have jurisdiction over "all civil actions arising under the Constitution, laws, or treaties of the United States."

2. Although cases to be decided under federal question jurisdiction have never been precisely defined, most cases will have federal law as the source of the cause of action.

3. Claims created by state law that require interpretation of a federal law do NOT fall within federal question jurisdiction.

C. Diversity

1. Amount in Controversy

    a. This rule does not apply to federal question cases.

    b. The party seeking federal jurisdiction must show that his claim was made in good faith and that it is possible the amount in controversy is over $50,000. The party is not required to prove the actual value of the amount in controversy.

    c. The party challenging the jurisdiction will only prevail if he shows with "legal certainty" that the claim will be adjudicated for less than $50,000.

    d. Jurisdiction may not be challenged if the actual recovery turns out to be less than $50,000.

    e. Under the majority rule, the amount at stake must be $50,000 to either the plaintiff or the defendant.

     f. Multiple plaintiffs or defendants:

         i. One plaintiff may aggregate several claims against a single defendant to reach the $50,000 minimum.

        ii. One plaintiff may not aggregate several claims against several defendants nor may he join claims against other defendants when he has aggregated several claims against one defendant to reach the minimum.

       iii. Multiple plaintiffs will qualify for federal jurisdiction when at least one plaintiff's claim is valued at $50,000.

       iv. Jurisdiction will be denied when several plaintiffs' claims total $50,000 but no single claim is $50,000. Exception: Two or more plaintiffs enforcing the same right or interest that they share or own.

       v. The same rules apply for class action suits.

       vi. A counterclaim may satisfy the $50,000 requirement.

  2. <u>D</u>iversity of Citizenship

     a. Complete Diversity
Each plaintiff must be from a different state than each defendant. However, co-plaintiffs and co-defendants may be citizens from the same state.

     b. Minimal Diversity
In federal interpleader cases, there is diversity where one or more plaintiffs is from a different state than one or more of the defendants.

     c. Citizenship is determined at the time the suit is brought, not at the time of the event in controversy.

D.   Enumerated Areas

   1. Constitution
     The Constitution enumerates various areas where the federal courts have original jurisdiction, such as admiralty and cases involving ambassadors and public ministers. None of these cases require a minimum amount in controversy.

   2. Statutes
     Congress has also passed statutes granting federal courts exclusive and original jurisdiction over certain areas of the law, including patent and copyright law, antitrust law, and cases where the United States is a party. With the exception of cases where the United States is a defendant, no amount in controversy requirement need be met.

E.   Supplemental Jurisdiction

   1. Traditional View
     Prior to the passage of the Federal Judiciary Act of 1991, state claims and parties, which would otherwise have to be adjudicated in a state court due to lack of federal subject matter jurisdiction, might be joined with a valid federal claim by virtue of notions known as pendent and ancillary jurisdiction.

     a. Pendent Jurisdiction
       By filing a state claim at the same time as a federal claim, and petitioning the federal court to hear both claims, a party is attempting to append the state claim to the federal claim.

     b. Ancillary Jurisdiction
       By petitioning a federal court presently hearing a valid federal claim to attach a state claim onto the federal proceeding, a party is requesting the court assert ancillary jurisdiction. The distinction between the two is largely academic because the rules governing both

types of jurisdiction are identical, and in any event, they have both been rendered moot by the supplemental jurisdiction statute.

c. Rules for Pendent/Ancillary Jurisdiction
As long as the state and federal claims derive from a "common nucleus of operative facts," the state and the federal claim may both be litigated in federal court, unless:

  i. The federal claim is dismissed before trial, or

  ii. The federal claim is based solely on diversity, and diversity does not exist with regards to the state claim (*United States v. Finley*).

2. Supplemental Jurisdiction
To correct what many perceived as the Supreme Court's misinterpretation of pendent and ancillary jurisdiction, Congress in 1991 enacted 28 U.S.C. § 1367.

a. What is Covered? (28 U.S.C. § 1367 (a))
Federal courts may now hear almost any claim that is transactionally related to a claim that is properly before the court. "Transactionally related" means that the supplemental claim arises out of the same transaction, occurrence or series of transactions or occurrences as the claim properly before the court.

b. What is not Covered? (28 U.S.C. § 1367 (b))
Claims brought by impleaded parties (FRCP 14), necessary parties (FRCP 19), indispensable parties (FRCP 20) and intervenors (FRCP 24) may not be attached to an existing diversity claim unless there is independent satisfaction of the diversity and amount in controversy requirements.

c. Discretionary Dismissal (28 U.S.C. § 1367 (c))
Even if a claim is not prohibited under § 1367 (b), a court may still dismiss a supplemental claim at its discretion if:

Mnemonic: **POND**

i. **P**redominating State Claim
When the state claim predominates over the federal case it would be more fair to have a state court decide the case.

ii. **O**ther Compelling Reasons
The statute requires "exceptional circumstances," but it has yet to be seen how rigid this requirement is.

iii. **N**ovel or Complex State Law
State courts are more qualified that federal courts to develop novel issues of state law.

iv. **D**ismissal of Federal Claims
The courts will be wary of using fraudulent diversity claims simply to get around federal jurisdiction requirements.

III. PERSONAL JURISDICTION

A. In Personam

1. Physical Presence

a. *Pennoyer v. Neff* (S.Ct. 1877)
A state court cannot assert in personam jurisdiction over a defendant unless the defendant was personally served with process in the state or the defendant voluntarily appeared before the court. But a state court may exercise jurisdiction over a defendant's property,

even if the property is not related to the action at hand, if the property is located within the court's jurisdiction.

b. Kinds of Jurisdiction:

   i. In Personam
      Personal service on the defendant within the state.

   ii. In Rem
      Attachment of defendant's in-state property when the defendant is out of state.

c. Momentary Presence
Jurisdiction may be asserted over any person entering the state for even a brief moment such as persons passing through by car or flying over in a plane.

2. Domicile

a. Defined
A court has in personam jurisdiction over an individual, even if the person is not physically present within the jurisdiction, provided that person was domiciled within the court's jurisdiction.

b. Determination
Domicile is determined by:

   i. A party's intent to permanently locate there, and

   ii. An affirmative act expressing such intent.

c. Limitation
A person may only have one domicile, even if he has more than one residence.

3. Jurisdiction Based On Consent

   a. A court may render a binding enforceable judgment against a party who consents to the jurisdiction of the court even if the court would not have had jurisdiction over the individual absent his consent.

   b. Kinds of Consent

      i. Express Consent

         (1) Defendant stipulates court's jurisdiction in advance of litigation.

         (2) Parties to a contract may specify jurisdiction in case of a dispute.

         (3) Parties to a contract appoint an in-state agent to accept process.

         (4) An appearance or filing of a motion will constitute express consent.

      ii. Implied Consent
           State statutes may specify that persons engaging in certain activities will impliedly consent to that state's jurisdiction.

      iii. Motorist Statutes
            In *Hess v. Pawloski* (1927), the Supreme Court validated a state statute conferring implied consent to jurisdiction upon any motorist operating a vehicle within the state.

4. Jurisdiction Over Corporations

   a. A corporation is subject to the jurisdiction of the state in which it is incorporated.

b. Fine Line Distinction
For in personam jurisdiction, a corporation is resident in the state in which it is incorporated. For federal diversity purposes, a corporation is considered resident in both its state of incorporation and the state where it maintains its principal place of business.

c. Unlike an individual, a corporation will not fall under a state's jurisdiction by the mere presence within the state of a corporate employee or officer.

5. Minimum Contacts Rule

a. *International Shoe Co. v. Washington*
In order to subject a defendant to in personam jurisdiction in a state where the defendant is neither domiciled nor present, there must be certain minimum contacts between the defendant and the forum such that maintenance of the suit does not offend traditional notions of fair play and substantial justice.

b. Two-Step Analysis

i. Does the defendant have minimum contacts with the forum? If so,

ii. Will asserting jurisdiction comply with traditional notions of fair play and justice?

c. *Hanson v. Denckla*
Jurisdiction may not be invoked when a defendant's contact with a forum is negligible and not purposeful.

d. *McGee v. International Life Insurance Co.*
A defendant's activities in a forum may subject the defendant to personal jurisdiction, even if there was only sporadic contact or a single act, as long as the action arises from that single act.

e. *Helicopteros Nacionales de Colombia, S.A. v. Hall*
The Court recognized a distinction made by some
courts between "general" and "specific" jurisdiction.

  i. Specific jurisdiction
  Defendant's presence in the forum jurisdiction is
  sporadic but the cause of action arose from a contact.

  ii. General jurisdiction
  Regular activity that will subject a party to a forum's jurisdiction even if the action did not arise
  from in-state activity. General jurisdiction may only
  be asserted when the defendant had substantial
  forum-related activity.

f. *Kulko v. Superior Court*
A parent does not establish minimum contacts with a
state by allowing a child to live with the other parent
in the forum state.

g. *World-Wide Volkswagen v. Woodson*
Conduct in a forum, not expectation of revenue, is how
jurisdiction is determined. The fact that the defendant
derived revenue from use of its product in the forum
state was not sufficient to confer jurisdiction.

h. *Asahi Metal Industry v. Superior Court*
Actions that are not purposefully directed toward the
forum state do not confer jurisdiction.

i. *Burger King v. Rudzewicz*
Jurisdiction is not conferred because one party to a
contract resides in the forum.

B.   In Rem Jurisdiction

1. Definitions

a. In Rem Jurisdiction
Jurisdiction based on a court's power over a thing, not a person. The action is technically against the property, not a person. The subject of the litigation is related to the property.

b. Quasi In Rem Jurisdiction
Jurisdiction based on an action against a person. Since the court is unable to obtain jurisdiction against the defendant, jurisdiction is obtained by seizing the defendant's property. The property is NOT related to the action. The action is against the person not the property. Had the court been able to obtain jurisdiction against the defendant, the action would have been based upon in personam jurisdiction. Quasi in rem actions may force the sale of real property, garnishment of wages, or assignment of a debt.

2. *Rush v. Savchuk*
Quasi in rem jurisdiction over an insurer may not be based on its obligation to defend a policy holder.

3. *Shaffer v. Heitner*
Quasi in rem jurisdiction may only be asserted when the defendant has the "minimum contacts" with the forum state that would satisfy the requirements for in personam jurisdiction as defined by *International Shoe*. The effect of this case is to almost eliminate the availability of quasi in rem jurisdiction. *Shaffer* blurred the difference between in rem and quasi in rem jurisdiction.

IV. NOTICE AND OPPORTUNITY TO BE HEARD

A. Generally
A court that has proper jurisdiction over a case may only proceed when the defendant has proper notice of the proceedings against him. Proper notice usually entails service of "process" consisting of a summons to appear and a copy of the complaint. The defendant need not necessarily receive actual notice of the suit but the procedures followed must be "reasonably likely" to provide notice. The defendant must have adequate time to prepare his defense.

B. Methods of Service

1. In Hand Service
Defendant is physically handed a summons.

2. Attachment
Defendant receives notice by the attachment of his tangible property. Statutes typically require additional notice such as mailing the summons or publication.

3. Garnishment
Garnishment of a debt or other nontangible property will satisfy the notice requirement in quasi in rem cases. Statutes require that further notice be provided.

4. Substituted Service
Modern statutes often allow substituted service so that justice will reach a defendant avoiding "hand service." Some types of substituted service generally allowed:

a. Mail

b. Summons affixed to door of the defendant's unattended dwelling

c. Summons left at defendant's dwelling

d. Court order

e. Summons left with a person of "suitable age and discretion" residing in the same dwelling as the defendant

5. Constructive Notice

a. Registered or certified mail

b. Publication

6. Corporations

a. Designated Corporate Official
The statute will designate the official to receive process.

b. *Mullane* Rule
Expense and availability of the names and addresses of the beneficiaries to numerous small trust funds should be taken into account in determining the sufficiency of notice by publication. Subsequent cases have required notice by mail to all parties.

V.   REMOVAL

A.   Generally
A defendant may remove an action to a federal court when the action had original federal jurisdiction but was filed in a state court.

B.   Exception
A diversity action may only be removed when neither party is a citizen of the state in which the action was asserted.

C.   Defendant's Right
Only the defendant may remove an action.

D. Valid State Jurisdiction Necessary
The state court's jurisdiction must be valid for removal jurisdiction to be valid.

VI. CHALLENGES TO JURISDICTION

A. Special Appearance

1. Traditional View
Since presence is one way of asserting jurisdiction over a party, without special appearance, any appearance in court, even to challenge jurisdiction, would invite a court to assert jurisdiction over the party. With special appearance a party appears only to challenge jurisdiction. If the challenge is successful, the case is dismissed, and the suit must be refiled with a new assertion of jurisdiction. If the challenge fails, the party is still present to challenge the merits of the case.

2. Modern View
Special appearance has been superseded by federal and other courts. In these courts, a defendant may now challenge jurisdiction by filing a motion to dismiss for lack of jurisdiction without being subject to jurisdiction for filing the motion. Many courts also allow a special appearance for in rem and quasi in rem actions.

B. Collateral Attack
A defendant defaulting on an action may collaterally attack a default judgement asserted in another jurisdiction on the grounds that the first action was asserted in a forum without proper jurisdiction. This often occurs where an award granted in one jurisdiction is to be enforced in a second jurisdiction.

VII. VENUE

A. Defined
The place within a jurisdiction where an action is brought.

B.   State and Local Courts
     Local rules establish venue. The location where the cause of
     action arose, residence, place of business of the defendant
     and plaintiff, and other factors are usually considered.

C.   Federal Venue
     Federal Venue shall be where defendants reside or where the
     claim arose. A corporation may be sued where incorporated,
     licensed to do business, or where it actually does business.
     An alien may be sued in any district.

D.   Forum Non Conveniens
     A court may decline jurisdiction over a case if it decides that
     the case should be tried elsewhere.

CASE CLIPS

Pennoyer v. Neff (S.Ct. 1877)

Facts: Mitchell brought an action against Neff in an Oregon court
to recover legal fees. By publication he served Neff, a nonresident,
and obtained judgment by default. Thereafter, Neff learned of the
sale of his property in Oregon to satisfy the judgment. He sued
Pennoyer, the purchaser, in Oregon to recover his property. Neff
argued that the Oregon court had no jurisdiction over him.

Issue: Is service by publication sufficient to give a state court in
personam jurisdiction over a nonresident?

Rule: (Field, J.)   A personal judgment against a nonresident
served only by publication is invalid. For personal jurisdiction (as
opposed to in rem jurisdiction over property) the defendant must
come within the court's jurisdiction by personal service within the
state or by voluntarily submitting himself to service of process. In
rem jurisdiction may be achieved by attaching the in-state property
of an out-of-state defendant who otherwise could not be brought
into the jurisdiction by in personam jurisdiction.

Dissent: (Hunt, J.) The states have the exclusive power to determine what notice is required to prospective defendants. As long as
that notice is "reasonably likely" to communicate notice of the suit,

is made in a good faith effort to notify him, and the defendant receives an opportunity to defend himself, the notice statute should be valid.

International Shoe Co. v. Washington
(S.Ct. 1945)

Facts: The state of Washington brought suit to collect unemployment taxes from a company that did not have an office in Washington and that was incorporated in another state, but which did have a sales force of 11 to 13 people in Washington who regularly solicited business.

Issue: What contacts are required for the courts of a state to exercise in personam jurisdiction over a nonresident defendant?

Rule: (Stone, C.J.) The courts of a state may exercise in personam jurisdiction over a nonresident defendant where that defendant has "the minimum contacts with the forum state such that maintenance of the suit does not offend traditional notions of fair play and substantial justice." It suffices that the defendant conducts systematic and continuous activities that relate to the obligation sued upon in the forum state.

Concurrence: (Black, J.) The Court should not be able to invalidate an otherwise valid state jurisdiction statute because of a foggy notion of "fair play."

Shaffer v. Heitner (S.Ct. 1977)

Facts: Heitner brought a shareholder's derivative suit against Greyhound and 28 of its officers and directors in Delaware, where Greyhound was incorporated, alleging that the corporation and its officers and directors (including Shaffer) were the cause of Greyhound's loss in an antitrust action in Oregon. Jurisdiction was based on sequestration of Shaffer's Greyhound stock, which was deemed, pursuant to Delaware state law, to be located in Delaware.

Issue: Absent other contacts of a defendant with a state, will sequestration of property deemed to be located in the state provide a state court with a basis for quasi in rem jurisdiction over an individual?

Rule: (Marshall, J.) Property which is not itself the subject matter of the litigation does not alone provide a basis for jurisdiction. The exercise of jurisdiction over the interests of persons is consistent with the Due Process Clause only where the "minimum contacts" standard of *International Shoe* is met.

Concurrence 1: (Powell, J.) Some types of property may allow some quasi in rem cases to comport with "traditional notions of fair play and substantial justice."

Concurrence 2: (Stevens, J.) The majority goes too far in invalidating much of in rem and quasi in rem jurisdiction.

Dissent: (Brennan, J.) Jurisdiction over officers involved in a corporation subject to a shareholder derivative action should be able to be conferred via the traditional "minimum contacts" test. It is not unreasonable for an officer to believe that he may have to defend his actions as corporate officer in the state of incorporation. Minimum contacts is not best contacts.

Note: *Shaffer* extends the "minimum contacts" rule of *International Shoe* so as to overrule part of the implied holding of Pennoyer v. Neff regarding in rem actions.

World-Wide Volkswagen Corporation v. Woodson
(S.Ct. 1980)

Facts: The Woodsons of New York bought an Audi in New York. After they were injured in a crash while driving through Oklahoma, they brought an action in Oklahoma against the New York dealer and the New York distributor of the car for defective design. Jurisdiction was based on the Oklahoma long-arm statute.

Issue: May a state exercise personal jurisdiction over a nonresident corporation who places its products into a "stream of commerce" that happens to place some of those products in the state?

Rule: (White, J.) The forum state may not exercise personal jurisdiction over a nonresident corporation whose product is "fortuitously" in the forum state, and whose conduct and connection with the forum are so attenuated that it would not reasonably anticipate becoming subject to the forum state's jurisdiction.

Dissent 1: (Brennan, J.) Given the nature of the automobile business, it is foreseeable that a car sold in New York may pass through Oklahoma, so jurisdiction should not be denied.

Dissent 2: (Marshall, J.) If a product enters the forum state through the intended use of the purchaser, that state should be able to assert jurisdiction over the product's manufacturer.

Dissent 3: (Blackmun, J.) Since "we are a nation on wheels" it is not unreasonable for a manufacturer of automobiles to be brought to any state where an accident involving one of its automobiles occurs.

Burger King Corporation v. Rudzewicz
(S.Ct. 1985)

Facts: Rudzewicz, a Michigan resident, entered an agreement with Burger King, a Florida corporation, to operate a franchise in Michigan. The contract stated that Florida law controlled and required monthly payments to be made to the corporation's headquarters in Florida. When Rudzewicz fell behind on his monthly obligations, Burger King brought suit in Florida.

Issue: May the forum state exercise in personam jurisdiction over a nonresident defendant who has entered into a contract with a corporation from the forum state?

Rule: (Brennan, J.) The forum state may exercise in personam jurisdiction over a nonresident defendant who has established a substantial and continuing relationship with a corporation from the forum state and received fair notice from the contract documents and the course of dealing that he might be subject to suit in the forum state.

Dissent: (Stevens, J.) A boilerplate contract should not be the basis for conferring jurisdiction over defendants with no contact with the forum state.

Asahi Metal Industry Co. v. Superior Court.
(S.Ct. 1987)

Facts: In a personal injury suit, Zurcher, a Californian, sued Cheng Shin, a tube-manufacturing company from Taiwan. The company, in turn, filed a cross-claim and sought indemnification from Asahi Metal, the Japanese manufacturer of the component part. Zurcher and Cheng Shin subsequently settled, leaving only the suit between Cheng Shin and Asahi.

Issue: Is the "minimum contacts" requirement for personal jurisdiction satisfied when a foreign corporation manufactures products outside the United States that end up in the forum state via the stream of commerce?

Rule: (O'Connor, J.) The "minimum contacts" test is not always satisfied when a component part manufactured outside the United States is later introduced into the stream of commerce. Assertion of jurisdiction must have been reasonably contemplated by the defending party, based on the defendant's interest in the forum state, the burden on the defendant to go to the forum, and the plaintiff's interest in obtaining relief.

Concurrence 1: (Brennan, J.) Although conferring jurisdiction over Asahi would not comport with "traditional notions of fair play and substantial justice," Asahi did have sufficient minimum contacts with the forum state. That a defendant may foresee that its products may enter the forum state via the stream of commerce should be sufficient. A stream of commerce is purposeful and directed, its outcome fairly predictable.

Concurrence 2: (Stevens, J.) Asahi certainly has minimum contacts with California, even if asserting jurisdiction in this case would be "unreasonable and unfair." Asahi, by dealing with Cheng Shin, knowing that a substantial portion of its business goes to California, has purposely availed itself of the forum state.

Burnham v. Superior Court (S.Ct. 1990)

Facts: Mr. and Mrs. Burnham lived in New Jersey. Mrs. Burnham moved to California with their children. When Mr. Burnham went to California to conduct business and visit the children, he was served with a California summons and a copy of Mrs. Burnham's divorce petition. He moved to quash the service of process on the grounds that the court lacked personal jurisdiction over him because his only contacts with California were a few short visits.

Issue: May a court exert jurisdiction over a non-resident who is personally served with process while temporarily in a state, in a suit unrelated to his activities in that state?

Rule: (Scalia, J.) Physical presence alone is sufficient for a state to exercise jurisdiction over a person; Due Process requirements are satisfied. Continuous and systematic contacts with the forum are not necessary. The litigation need not arise out of activities within the state.

Dissent: (Brennan, J.) The Due Process clause generally permits state courts to exercise jurisdiction over a defendant while he is voluntarily present in a state.

Insurance Corp. of Ireland, Ltd. v. Compagnie des Bauxites de Guinee (S.Ct. 1982)

Facts: The Compagnie des Bauxites de Guinee of Delaware sued Insurance Corp. of Ireland and several other foreign "excess insurers" in a diversity action in Pennsylvania, alleging breach of an insurance contract guaranteed by Insurance Corp. and the excess investors. During discovery, Insurance Corp. failed to produce requested documents that might have proven sufficient contact with Pennsylvania to allow the court to assert federal jurisdiction. Pursuant to FRCP 37(b)(2)(A), the court issued an order compelling production of the requested documents, warning that failure to produce documents would result in the court presuming valid in personam jurisdiction.

Issue: May a court presume a valid assertion of jurisdiction pursuant to FRCP 37(b)(2)(A) due to a party's failure to produce requested documents during discovery?

Rule: (White, J.) Imposing a sanction pursuant to FRCP 37(b)(2)-(A) for a party's failure to comply with discovery requests that a "finding" of personal jurisdiction over the party exists will not violate due process. The party's failure to produce requested documents in such situations allows the court to presume jurisdiction.

Concurrence: (Powell, J.) Rule 37(b) does not create a broader standard for jurisdiction. A court may not issue Rule 37(b) sanctions without first establishing that "minimum contacts" exist, even if the sanctions relate to that establishment of "minimum contacts."

National Equipment Rental, Ltd. v. Szukhent (S.Ct. 1964)

Facts: Szukhent of Michigan leased farm equipment from National Equipment Rental, Ltd. of New York. The contract provided that attorney Florence Weinberg would accept service in New York for claims arising from the contract. When Szukhent defaulted on payment, Weinberg was served, and she mailed the complaint to Szukhent.

Issue: When may a party to a private contract appoint an agent to receive service of process?

Rule: (Stewart, J.) A party to a private contract may agree that any litigation under the contract shall be conducted in a particular state and may appoint an agent to receive service of process, even if the agent is not personally known to the party and the agent has not expressly undertaken to transmit notice to the party.

Dissent: (Black, J.) Service of process to an agent should not be valid, no matter how it is developed. Although there is no due process issue in this case because the defendant did receive actual notice of the summons and complaint, the possibility for abuse of such clauses exists where large companies may force customers to come to a forum state the seller prefers.

Mullane v. Central Hanover Bank & Trust Co.
(S.Ct. 1950)

Facts: Known and unknown nonresident beneficiaries of a trust fund were given notice of the application for judicial settlement of the account by publication in a local newspaper.

Issue: Is notice by publication of the pendency of an action adequate when attempting to inform known parties who could be apprised more effectively by mail or other means?

Rule: (Jackson, J.) The fundamental requisite of due process is the opportunity to be heard. Due process requires that notice be reasonably calculated to apprise interested parties. Notice by publication to known nonresidents is inadequate because it is not reasonably calculated to reach those who could easily be informed by other means.

Dissent: (Burton, J.) The Constitution does not require more notice than that presently provided by statute here.

Omni Capital International v. Rudolf Wolff & Co. Ltd.
(S.Ct. 1987)

Facts: Two New York corporations (collectively called "Omni"), marketed an investment program and employed a British corporation with London offices to manage trades on that Exchange. In an action in Louisiana, Omni impleaded both the British corporation and its representative arguing that their liability resulted from the representative's improprieties.

Issue: What are the prerequisites to a federal court's exercise of personal jurisdiction over a party?

Rule: (Blackmun, J.) A federal court can exercise personal jurisdiction over a party when there is a basis for the party's amenability to service of a summons, and if in addition, notice requirements and a nexus between the party and the forum state are established.

In re Union Carbide Corporation Gas Plant Disaster at Bhopal, India in December, 1984 (1987)

Facts: More than 2,000 people were killed after lethal gas escaped a chemical plant in India operated by Union Carbide, an American corporation. A month later, the government of India passed a law designating itself the sole representative of the victims. India then sued Union Carbide in federal court in New York. Union Carbide moved to dismiss to India on the ground of forum non conveniens. The district court granted the motion on the grounds that Union Carbide consent to Indian jurisdiction, agree to pay any decision that comports with minimal requirements of due process, and makes itself available to federal discovery rules.

Issue: May a court dismiss a suit on the ground of forum non conveniens subject to conditions?

Rule: A court may dismiss on the ground of forum non conveniens subject to a party consenting to jurisdiction, but may not put additional burdens that impugn the integrity of a foreign court's ability to conduct a fair trial (such as the latter two conditions).

Louisville & Nashville R.R. v. Mottley (S.Ct. 1908)

Facts: Mottley brought an action in federal court alleging that the opposing party had breached a contract by revoking a pass for free transportation. Mottley asserted federal question jurisdiction based on the railroad company's anticipated defense that an act of Congress proscribed free passes.

Issue: Does the anticipated assertion of federal law as a defense to an action suffice to provide federal question jurisdiction?

Rule: (Moody, J.) Only when a plaintiff's own cause of action states a federal question do federal courts have federal question jurisdiction.

Mas v. Perry (1974)

Facts: Jean Paul Mas of France and Judy Mas of Mississippi settled in Louisiana after their marriage without intending to remain there permanently. They brought a suit in federal court against Perry, a Mississippi resident, basing federal jurisdiction on diversity of citizenship.

Issue: Is mere "residence" in a state sufficient to establish state domicile so as to defeat or establish diversity?

Rule: For purpose of diversity, "domicile" is a permanent home, and requires intent to remain permanently in a state.

Note: In the instant case, neither Mas became a domiciliary of Louisiana, and there was complete diversity of citizenship.

United Mine Workers of America v. Gibbs (S.Ct. 1966)

Facts: Gibbs brought an action in federal court, asserting both a federal claim, under the Management Relations Act, and a state claim, conspiracy to interfere with a contract.

Issue: Do federal courts have jurisdiction to hear state claims if they are brought together with federal claims?

Rule: (Brennan, J.) Federal courts have discretion to assume pendent jurisdiction of state claims if they are brought together with substantial federal claims and are derived from a common nucleus of operative facts.

Willy v. Coastal Corp. (1988)

Facts: Willy filed suit against Coastal for wrongful discharge, alleging that they fired him because he refused to act in violation of state and federal environmental and securities laws. Coastal removed the case to federal court on the ground that some of the statutes Willy was asked to violate were federal. The federal statutes had a "whistleblower" provision that created an administrative remedy to protect informants from retributory firing. They were not intended to preempt state employment law.

Issue: May a defendant remove an action to federal court on the basis of federal question jurisdiction if there is a State cause of action that relies in part upon federal law?

Rule: A case may be removed to federal court if federal law completely preempts a state cause of action. A case may also be removed if federal law creates the cause of action or if the action requires resolution of a substantial question of federal law. The court found that Willy's suit could not be removed because 1) federal environmental and security laws are not meant to preempt wrongful discharge claims; 2) federal law created a cause of action only for "whistleblowers", which is not applicable to Willy; 3) federal courts, at any rate, could not hear a "whistleblower" claim because federal law only provides an administrative remedy; and 4) the federal element of Willy's claim is not substantial enough to confer federal question jurisdiction.

Chapter 3

THE ERIE PROBLEM

I.   INTRODUCTION

A.   Explanation
A common conflict arising from the federal system is determining what procedures to use when a state claim is asserted in federal courts, and when federal claims are asserted in state courts. Further complicating matters is the fuzzy line between procedure and substance. The *Erie* doctrine sets forth a framework, however convoluted, for determining which law to apply.

B.   Policy Considerations

1. Forum Shopping
Insofar as one procedural law might be more favorable to litigants than another, courts attempt to prevent litigants from using the federal courts as a method of finding the most favorable jurisdiction.

2. Uniformity
Having two sets of laws may create confusion among citizens, especially where one law may direct a citizen to do that which another law discourages.

3. Federalism
Despite the Supremacy Clause, federal courts are wary of treading too harshly on state autonomy in drafting their own substantive remedies.

4. States as Laboratories
State legislatures often take the initiative on various legislation that Congress may later incorporate into its own laws. Forcing uniformity may impede such inventiveness.

II. STATE LAW IN FEDERAL COURTS

A. History

  1. Rules of Decision Act
     Located in § 34 of the Judiciary Act of 1789, the Rules of Decisions Act directed federal courts to apply "the laws of the several states, except where the Constitution, treaties, or statutes of the United States shall otherwise require or provide. . . ."

  2. *Swift v. Tyson* (1842)
     Justice Story's decision held that:

     a. State law should be applied in federal court only when ruling on matters of purely local concern (e.g. real estate).

     b. Federal courts were free to evolve their own "general" common law regarding state laws.

  3. The Advent of Forum Shopping
     The creation of federal common law encouraged forum-shopping. Since litigants could choose between two distinct bodies of common law, the party would choose the forum with the most favorable law. This unsatisfactory state of affairs lasted for nearly a century.

B. *Erie Railroad Co. v. Tompkins* (1938)

  1. The Holding
     Justice Brandeis' decision ended the *Swift v. Tyson* era in its tracks. There the court:

     a. Held that state law, including both statutory and common law, must be applied to substantive issues in cases based on diversity jurisdiction.

      b. Expressly overruled *Swift v. Tyson* as "an unconstitutional assumption of powers by the Courts of the United States."

      c. Eradicated federal general common law.

   2. Underlying Policies

      a. Elimination of uncontrolled forum-shopping, and

      b. Avoidance of inequitable administration of laws.

   3. What *Erie* Did Not Change
     Federal law still applies in diversity cases when a federal statute or federal question is involved.

C.   Federal Procedural Laws

   1. The Conformity Act (1872)
     Federal courts must follow the procedure of the courts of the state in which it is located. This law has been replaced by the Enabling Act of 1934.

   2. Enabling Act (1934)
     The Supreme Court may now formulate general rules of procedure for the federal courts. The Act stated that the procedural rules were not to "abridge, enlarge, nor modify the substantive rights of any litigant." However, substance and procedure are not easy to distinguish.

   3. Federal Rules of Civil Procedure (1938 — same year as *Erie*) provided general rules of procedure in accordance with the Enabling Act.

D.   Scope of the *Erie* Decision
    Following *Erie*, the Supreme Court formulated a series of tests to help the federal courts decide whether a given state law is substantive or procedural.

1. *York* Outcome-Determinative Test
   In *Guaranty Trust Co. v. York* (1945), a federal court in a diversity case should apply state law if the federal procedural rule would lead to a substantially different result. The court in *Guaranty* applied the state statute of limitations, finding it substantive for *Erie* purposes.

2. *Byrd* Balancing Test
   In *Byrd v. Blue Ridge Rural Electric Cooperative, Inc.* (1958), Justice Brennan's decision held that the preference for state law must be balanced against denial of the federal right. If a state law in a diversity action would deny a party a strongly-protected federal right, the federal rule or policy should be followed even if it would lead to a substantially different outcome.

3. *Hanna* "Smart Person" Test
   In *Hanna v. Plumer* (1965), Chief Justice Warren set out what is currently the definitive test for ascertaining the applicable law.

   a. Presumption of Procedure
      State laws are presumed to be procedural. Thus, federal rules must be followed to the exclusion of a state law if the federal rule is sanctioned by the Rules Enabling Act.

      i. It does not "abridge, enlarge, nor modify the substantive rights of any litigant."

      ii. Note that no federal rule has yet been held to infringe on a litigant's rights. This is due in part to Chief Justice Warren's assertion that the FRCP were enacted by "smart people" who would know better.

b. Conflict With the State Law

i. Direct Conflict
If the federal rule is in direct conflict with the law of the state, the federal rule must still be followed.

ii. Indirect Conflict
Even if there is no direct conflict with state procedural law, the federal rule will preclude the use of a state statute if it occupies the field of operation of the state statute (see *Burlington Northern Railroad Co. v. Woods*).

iii. No Conflict
If there is no conflict at all, or if the rule in question is not in the FRCP, *Hanna* does not apply.

(1) Some courts employ the analysis of *Erie* and the balancing test of *Byrd*.

(2) Justice Scalia, dissenting in *Stewart Organization Inc. v. Ricoh*, would prefer to apply the *York* outcome determinative test, but his approach does not yet command a majority of the court. Several lower courts have applied *York*, however.

(3) Some courts have held that *Hanna* has overruled *Byrd*, and that unless a rule is in the FRCP, state law must apply, and if it is in the FRCP, the federal and state rules will be applied simultaneously.

4. The Harlan Concurrence
Justice Harlan's concurrence in *Hanna v. Plumer* provided a stricter test. In deciding whether to apply a state or federal rule, a court must determine if the choice of rule would substantially affect those primary decisions respecting human conduct that our constitutional system leaves to state regulation. So far, this test has had no impact on

the law, although it has been supported by several scholars.

E.   The Problem of Ascertaining State Law
Federal courts adjudicating a state claim must predict how the highest court of the state would decide the claim.

1.   State Authority
Statutes and Constitutions of the state must be applied as interpreted by the state's highest court. If there is no holding in the highest court, lower court decisions should be consulted as persuasive authority.

2.   Certification
The question may be certified to the state's highest court.

3.   Analogy
If the issue has not been undertaken by the state before, other authorities may be consulted to help discern how the highest court would rule. Federal courts can also consider analogous rulings and policies if the most recent case law on point is outdated or unclear.

4.   Conflicts of Law
Federal courts must also apply the conflicts of laws rules of the state in which it is sitting (see *Klaxon v. Stentor Elec. Mfg. Co.*).

F.   Residual Federal Common Law
Even though Erie declares "there is no federal general common law," there are situations where federal common law is employed to avoid subjecting strong federal interests to the inconsistencies of the laws of the several states.

1.   Federal common law is followed in most federal question cases:

Mnemonic: **FLUID**

a. **F**oreign relations matters.

b. Federal statute of **L**imitations applied where analogous state statutes of limitations either do not exist, or do not adequately protect the interests Congress wished to protect.

c. **U**nited States is a party.

d. **I**nterpreting federal statutes, treaties, or the Constitution.

e. **D**isputes between the states.

2. Federal common law is also followed in some diversity cases:

a. Federal defense is raised, or

b. Federal interests outweigh state interests. Incidental federal concerns are not sufficient to compel the use of federal common law in a purely private litigation (see *Bank of America Nat. Trust & Sav. Ass'n v. Parnell*).

III. FEDERAL LAW IN STATE COURTS (REVERSE *ERIE*)

A. Supremacy Clause
When a federal claim is brought in a state court, the Supremacy Clause of the Constitution (Art. VI) compels the application of federal law.

B. Federal Defense
A federal right may be relevant to a state action if it is interposed as a defense to a state action.

C.   Superseding State Law
State rules of procedure must not be followed if they impose unnecessary burdens on federal rights of recovery (see *Brown v. Western Ry. of Alabama*).

CASE CLIPS

Erie Railroad Co. v. Tompkins (S.Ct. 1938)

Facts: As Tompkins walked on Erie Railroad Company's land, a freight train injured him. While Pennsylvania common law would have denied Tompkins relief as a trespasser, federal common law did not regard Tompkins a trespasser. No Pennsylvania statute applied to the issue of trespassing. In *Swift v. Tyson* (S.Ct. 1842), Justice Story held that the Federal Judiciary Act required federal courts to apply state statutes, but not state common law, in diversity cases. Accordingly, the District Court applied federal common law in this diversity case and awarded damages to Tompkins.

Issue: Which law, federal or state, must be applied to substantive issues arising in a diversity case?

Rule: (Brandeis, J.) Under the Constitution, only state law, both common law and statutory law, may be applied to substantive issues arising in a diversity case. There is no federal general common law.

Concurrence: (Reed, J.) This case need only be decided by expanding the word "law" in § 34 of the Federal Judiciary Act to include common law as well as statutes. Absent the Federal Judiciary Act, it is unclear whether federal courts may, under the Constitution, develop their own common law.

Dissent: (Butler, J.) Since no finding of the railroad's negligence was ever made, the case should be retried. Furthermore, by forcing courts to adhere to state law, the majority infringes on Congress' ability to regulate the federal court system.

Guaranty Trust Co. v. York (S.Ct. 1945)

Facts: York, who could not sue in state court because the statute of limitations had run, brought suit in federal district court against the Guaranty Trust Company, alleging a breach of fiduciary duty. York claimed that the statute of limitations was a procedural matter to be governed by federal law. The court of appeals ruled that the fact that the action was brought in equity meant that the federal court could disregard the state rule.

Issue: When is a federal court that is hearing a state claim in a diversity case bound by state law?

Rule: (Frankfurter, J.) A federal court in a diversity case should follow the state rule if ignoring state law would lead to a substantially different result than if the suit had been brought in state court. Using this "outcome-determinative" test, the Court applied the state statute of limitations, finding it substantive for *Erie* purposes.

Dissent: (Rutledge, J.) Whether or not the action may be barred depends not upon the law of the state which creates the substantive right, but upon the law of the state where suit may be brought.

Byrd v. Blue Ridge Rural Electric Cooperative, Inc. (S.Ct. 1958)

Facts: After being injured on the job, Byrd brought a federal diversity action against his employer, Blue Ridge Electric, alleging negligence. A state workmen's compensation statute gave certain employers immunity from suit. Under state law a judge, not the jury, decides whether an employer fits within the statute's immunity. In the federal action, the jury decided all the factual issues, including whether Blue Ridge fit within the statute's immunity.

Issue: Should a federal court sitting in diversity follow a federal rule or policy even though the suit would lead to a substantially different outcome had it been prosecuted in state court?

Rule: (Brennan, J.) A federal rule or policy should be applied to the exclusion of state law that would mandate a different result where the federal interest at stake outweighs any countervailing state interest, coupled with the desire for uniform application of the laws. Applying this "balancing test," the court found that the federal interest in jury decisions outweighed the state's interest in uniform application of the law. But the court remanded the case to allow Blue Ridge to introduce evidence showing it fit within the statutory immunity.

Hanna v. Plumer (S.Ct. 1965)
Facts: Osgood and Hanna of Ohio were involved in an auto accident in South Carolina. Hanna of Ohio sued Plumer, executor of Osgood's estate, in a federal diversity action in Plumer's home district of Massachusetts. In compliance with FRCP 4(d)(1), copies of the summons and complaint were left with Plumer's wife at his residence. Plumer moved for summary judgement on the ground that service was not sufficient because the complaint was not personally served upon him, as required by Massachusetts state law.
Issue: Must a federal court sitting in diversity follow an applicable federal rule despite a conflicting state law, even if the outcome of the diversity suit will be altered thereby?
Rule: (Warren, C.J.) Where federal procedure and state law conflict, only the federal procedure will be applied in federal court. A federal law is procedural if it has been validly enacted under the Federal Enabling Act, and does not violate constitutional principles. Where they do not conflict, the *York* "outcome-determinative" test should be applied to determine whether the federal rule should be applied at all.
Concurrence: (Harlan, J.) State rules should be applied in lieu of a contrary federal rule where the state law directs a "private primary activity." This state law does not address any primary interest.

Stewart Organization, Inc. v. Ricoh Corp. (S.Ct. 1988)
Facts: Stewart, Inc., an Alabama corporation, entered into a dealership agreement with Ricoh Corp., a New Jersey corporation. Stewart later sued Ricoh in a federal diversity suit in Alabama for breach of contract. Ricoh petitioned the court for a transfer of venue, under 28 U.S.C. § 1404, to the southern district of New York, as specified in the contract's forum selection clause. The district court denied the transfer because of Alabama's strong interest against transfers of venue.

Issue: Should a federal court sitting in diversity apply state or federal law in deciding whether to transfer venue?

Rule: (Marshall, J.) Since the federal venue transfer statute (mandating some consideration of the forum selection clause) and the state venue transfer statute (mandating no consideration of the forum selection clause) conflict, *Hanna v. Plumer* dictates that the federal statute controls.

Chapter 4

REMEDIES

I. INTRODUCTION

If one can establish before a court that he has a right that is being threatened or has been violated, he is entitled to an appropriate remedy. In fact, United States jurisprudence does not really recognize any rights unless there is an accompanying remedy. There are primarily two types of remedies: specific remedies and substitutionary remedies.

II. SPECIFIC V. SUBSTITUTIONARY REMEDIES

A. Specific Remedies
    Specific remedies seek to restore an aggrieved party to the actual position he would have been in had his right not been violated.

B. Substitutionary Remedies
    Substitutionary remedies seek to restore the plaintiff to an equivalent position, generally by awarding money damages deemed of equivalent value for the right that was lost. Substitutionary remedies are more common because in many situations, specific remedies are not available.

C. Distinguished
    For example, if someone unlawfully took possession of your house, the specific remedy would be to replevin the house to you. However, if someone unlawfully took possession of your house and burned it to the ground, they obviously cannot restore the house to you. A substitutionary remedy, such as the monetary equivalent, would be necessary.

III. INJUNCTIONS
    An injunction is an order for someone to do or refrain from doing something. Because it is a court order, violation is treated as contempt.

A. Injunction is appropriate if:

1. The plaintiff is being threatened by some injury for which he has no adequate legal remedy (i.e., money damages), and;

2. The hardship the plaintiff will endure if relief is denied outweighs the hardship the defendant will endure if relief is granted.

B. Preliminary Injunctions/ Provisional Remedies
Often, a situation develops where a plaintiff's right will be irreparably lost if immediate action is not taken to protect it. Common examples are the threatened destruction of irreplaceable property, or fraudulent mismanagement of a corporation that threatens its continued existence.

On the other hand, due process demands that there be notice and an opportunity to be heard at a meaningful time and in a meaningful manner before property is taken.

There are two tests that are commonly employed to resolve this tension:

1. Test One

a. The plaintiff will suffer irreparable injury if injunctive relief is not granted;

b. The plaintiff will *probably* prevail on the merits;

c. In balancing the equities, the defendants will not be harmed more than the plaintiff is helped by the injunction;

d. Granting the injunction is in the public interest.

2. Test Two:

    a. The harm that will occur to the plaintiff is very serious; and;

    b. There is a *fair* chance the plaintiff will prevail on the merits.

IV. OTHER REMEDIES

A. Liquidated Damages
It is often difficult to calculate the proper measure of damages necessary to vindicate a right. Consequently, the amount of damages is sometimes predetermined. The most common example of this is a liquidated-damages clause in a contract. With a liquidated damage clause, the parties agree among themselves what the proper measure of damages should be if either of them breaches, thereby avoiding speculation and easing the dolor of litigation costs. Courts will not enforce these clauses, however, if they are unreasonable.

B. Punitive Damages
Punitive damages are occasionally awarded on top of compensatory damages to discourage certain types of behavior.

C. Attorney's Fees
In the United States there is a strong policy against awarding attorney's fees, although there are a few limited circumstances where they are permitted by statute.

D. Declaratory Judgments.
A declaratory judgment is one in which a court defines the rights and legal relations of the interested parties, and determines whether any further relief is available. Declaratory judgments are not usually accompanied by direct orders.

CASE CLIPS

United States v. Hatahley (1958)

Facts: In connection with a lawsuit over grazing rights, federal agents rounded up Navajo livestock and sold it to a glue factory. This action violated of federal law. The district court awarded each Navajo plaintiff $395 per horse or burro, half the diminution of value of the herds of sheep, goats, and cattle, and $3500 for mental pain and suffering.

Issue: What is the proper measure of damages to compensate a party for destroyed chattel?

Rule: The fundamental principal of damages is to restore an injured party, as nearly as possible, to the position he would have been in had it not been for the wrong of the other party. In this case, the plaintiffs were entitled to the market value or replacement cost of their horses and burros as of the time of taking, plus the use value of the animals between the time they were taken and the time that a reasonable person could have replaced them (e.g., lost profits because supplies could not be transported, etc.). Damages may be awarded for pain and suffering, but a fixed amount cannot be awarded to all plaintiffs. Because this is an individual matter, not a common injury, each plaintiff's pain and suffering must be separately evaluated.

Sigma Chemical Co. v. Harris (1985)

Facts: When Harris accepted employment with Sigma Chemical, he agreed not disclose any confidential information he learned at Sigma and that he would not work for any of Sigma's competitors for two years after leaving Sigma's employ. After becoming dissatisfied with Sigma, Harris accepted a job with one of Sigma's biggest competitors. Sigma brought suit to enjoin Harris from continuing to work for the competitor.

Issue: When is injunctive relief appropriate?

Rule: An injunction is appropriate if 1) the plaintiff is being threatened by some injury for which he has no adequate legal remedy (i.e., money damages), and 2) the hardship on the plaintiff if relief is denied outweighs the hardship the defendant will endure if relief is granted. The court found that Sigma was entitled to injunctive relief because Harris was in violation of the restrictive employment covenant, there was a strong threat that he would cause Sigma irreparable harm by disclosing trade secrets, Harris could easily find other employment, and Harris voluntarily violated the contract.

Marek v. Chesny (S.Ct. 1985)

Facts: While responding to a call, three police officers shot and killed Chesny's son. Chesny rejected a settlement of $100,000 that included attorney's fees. After receiving a jury award of only $60,-000, Chesny requested, under 42 U.S.C. § 1983, $171,692.47 in costs, including attorney's fees. The police contested the request under FRCP 68 which shifted the costs of trial, after the settlement offer had been made, to the plaintiff if a rejected settlement offer is greater than the trial award.

Issue 1: Under FRCP 68, must a rejected settlement offer separately list the amount included to cover costs?

Rule 1: (Burger, C.J.) Settlement offers are presumed to cover all costs, so there is no need to list the costs separately.

Issue 2: Under FRCP 68, do "costs" include attorney's fees?

Rule 2: FRCP 68 includes all costs properly awardable under the relevant statute. Although there is a general aversion in American courts to awarding attorney's fees, 42 U.S.C. § 1983 does explicitly include attorney's fees in "costs."

William Inglis & Sons Baking Co. v. ITT Continental Baking Co. (1976)

Facts: William Inglis & Sons Baking filed an antitrust action and requested a preliminary injunction against various competitors for below-cost pricing of bread products. The injunction was denied and Inglis appealed.

Issue: When should a court issue a preliminary injunction?

Rule: There are two tests that must be applied to determine whether a court should issue preliminary injunction. Test One: 1) the plaintiff will suffer irreparable injury if injunctive relief is not granted; 2) the plaintiff will *probably* prevail on the merits; 3) in balancing the equities, the defendants will not be harmed more than the plaintiff is helped by the injunction; 4) granting the injunction is in the public interest. Test Two: 1) the harm that will occur to the plaintiff is very serious; and 2) there is a *fair* chance the plaintiff will prevail on the merits. The court here remanded the case because the lower court failed to apply the second test.

Fuentes v. Shevin (S.Ct. 1972)

Facts: Fuentes purchased a stove and other household goods from Firestone under an installment conditional sales contract. When a dispute arose over the servicing of the stove, the seller sued for repossession of all of the goods. Before the complaint had been served on Fuentes, Goodyear obtained a writ of replevin authorizing the sheriff to seize the disputed goods at once. Fuentes challenged the state statute authorizing prejudgment replevin, for which Fuentes was offered neither notice nor a hearing in advance of seizure.

Issue: Do prejudgment replevin procedures that allow property to be seized without notice or an opportunity to challenge violate due process where a hearing is granted after the property is taken?

Rule: (Stewart, J.) It is fundamental to due process that there be notice and an opportunity to be heard at a meaningful time and in a meaningful manner before there is a significant taking of property by a state.

Dissent: (White, J.) In these situations the importance to the creditor of being able to repossess the items while they are still able to be located may outweigh the danger of an erroneous repossession.

Note: There are "extraordinary situations" which may justify postponing notice and opportunity for a hearing. First, the seizure must be directly necessary to secure an important governmental or general public interest. Second, there must a special need for prompt action.

Chapter 5

PLEADING

I. INTRODUCTION

A. Generally
    The purpose of pleadings under the Federal Rules is to give
    each party sufficient notice about a lawsuit. Under the Feder-
    al Rules, pleading the facts that serve as the basis for the
    complaint is not necessary; a claimant's verified impression
    of a fact will suffice.

B. Pleading Stages
    There are three pleading stages under the Federal Rules:

    1. Complaint
        Informs the defendant of the charges against him.

    2. Answer
        Alerts the plaintiff to the allegations in the complaint that
        the defendant will contest, as well as any existing counter-
        claims and affirmative defenses.

    3. Reply
        In the event of a counterclaim, serves the same function
        as the answer to the complaint.

II. THE DEVELOPMENT OF MODERN PLEADING

A. Historical Survey

    1. At the time of the Norman Conquest (1066) and for a
        century afterward, suitors resorted not to royal courts but
        to local and feudal courts. Royal courts handled offenses
        against the King's laws and did not interfere with the
        other courts.

2. Increasingly, people would seek justice from the King.

   a. A writ issued by the King was required for this.

   b. At first, the King drew each writ to fit a particular case.

   c. Patterns emerged and writs became standardized.

   d. By the twelfth century, a party could have justice done by the King if his case fit within the fixed formula of an existing writ.

3. Each writ came to embody a form of action which controlled

   a. The manner in which a suit was commenced.

   b. The substantive requirements of the case.

   c. The procedure of the trial.

   d. The remedies available.

4. Forms of Action

   a. Trespass
   A means of seeking damages from a party who had done violence to land, body, and/or property.

   b. Case
   Some trespass actions did not involve the direct application of unlawful force and evolved into an action on the "case."

      i. The law of negligence unfolded within this form of action.

  ii. Sometimes the line between trespass and case was not clear. One of the rules employed was that a trespass action was maintainable if an "immediate injury" resulted from the action.

 c. Other forms of action included debt, detinue, replevin, covenant, account, assumpsit, and trover.

B.   Common Law Pleading

 1. Objective
 To present a single issue for trial.

 2. Highly Technical System
 Required each pleading to be designed in accordance with a form of action that bound the party to one theory of substantive recovery.

 3. No Amendments
 Therefore an error in the pleadings would prove fatal to a complainant's case.

 4. Only Pretrial Procedure
 This necessitated the use of numerous pleadings and responses which wasted judicial time (now we have summary judgment, pretrial conferences, discovery, etc).

C.   Rise of Equity

 1. The Chancellor at the head of the Chancery drew up the writs for common law actions.

 2. By the fourteenth century, the Chancery was also granting remedies in equitable proceedings.

 3. Equity courts were entirely distinct from the common law courts and developed their own procedural methods and remedies.

4. Equitable relief was available if there was no adequate remedy at law. The court would be reluctant to fashion an equitable remedy if it was difficult to enforce or if it required detailed supervision.

5. Specific relief was obtainable through equity.

6. Equity courts could allow defenses or actions based on fraud, grant injunctions, or require specific performance. This was different from the common law courts which usually granted money damages.

7. Equity acted against the person so that a failure to satisfy a judgment could be enforced by fines and imprisonment. Since common law did not act against the person, the plaintiff would have to resort to additional measures if the defendant failed to satisfy a common law judgment.

D. Code Pleading
Modern Pleading originated with the 1848 New York Code of Civil Procedure, referred to as the "Field Code." The Code altered the old pleading structure in many ways:

1. Abolished forms of action so that the plaintiff could recover under any legal theory.

2. Merged law and equity.

   a. All civil courts could grant legal and equitable relief.

   b. The same procedure was to be used in all civil actions.

3. Emphasized factual pleadings

   a. The pleadings were to include only "ultimate facts" and not evidentiary facts or conclusions of law.

b. The difficulty in determining whether or not a pleading contained "ultimate facts" was the cause of much litigation.

4. Limited the pleadings to a complaint, answer, reply, and demurrers.

5. Required liberal construction of the pleadings so that cases would not be decided for technical reasons.

E. Theory of Pleadings
Many judges in Code states were reluctant to pull away too far from the rigidity of forms of action.

1. Required the judge to determine the single legal theory upon which the party relied.

2. If the facts pleaded did not support the legal theory, the cause of action could not be maintained and the party usually could not shift reliance to another legal theory of recovery.

3. Therefore, even in Code states, cases were still being decided for technical reasons.

F. Federal Rules of Civil Procedure

1. The Federal Rules of Civil Procedure were introduced in 1938.

2. The principal purpose of pleadings under the Federal Rules is to give notice to the other party of the nature of the lawsuit.

3. Formal pleading requirements have been eliminated. Much reliance is placed on pretrial discovery to develop the issues of the case.

4. Many states have modeled their codes after the Federal Rules.

III. THE COMPLAINT

The complaint, when filed by the plaintiff, commences a lawsuit.

A. Requirements
A valid complaint should include the proper:

1. Elements

   a. Jurisdictional basis for the claim.

   b. A statement of the claim.

   c. The relief sought.

2. Language
   The complaint need not be overly specific but should contain plain language (i.e., plaintiff need not specify which codes or statutes defendant allegedly violated). Thus, the defendant cannot say that the allegations were not technical enough or that he could not understand certain allegations.

B. Code Requirements
To be valid, a complaint must allege the material and ultimate facts upon which plaintiff's rights of action is based.

C. Federal Rules Requirements
Under FRCP 8(a) a complaint must contain the following:

1. A short and plain statement of the grounds upon which the court's jurisdiction depends.

2. A short and plain statement of the claim showing that the pleader is entitled to relief.

3. A demand for judgment for the relief the pleader seeks.

D. The Right to Relief
Under FRCP 8(a)(2), the pleader must show that he is entitled to relief. A complaint lacking a material element should not be dismissed if the plaintiff can prove the material element at trial.

E. Alternative and Inconsistent Allegations
FRCP 8(e)(2) permits alternate pleadings even when they are inconsistent. In the past, courts have held that pleadings containing inconsistent allegations are defective if they appear in a single cause of action or defense, but they have approved such inconsistent allegations when listed in separate causes of action or separate defenses. Most jurisdictions now permit inconsistent allegations whether or not separately stated. Several states have modified their pleading rules to permit inconsistent allegations.

F. Damages
FRCP 9(g) requires that special damages must be specifically stated. Moreover, special damages must be pleaded before evidence relating to such damages is introduced.

G. Relief
FRCP 8(a)(3) states that a complaint that claims a relief must contain a demand for judgment for the said relief. FRCP 54(c) states that a judgment by default shall not be different from or exceed the demand for the judgment. However, some courts have held that a claimant may be awarded damages in excess of those demanded in his pleadings if he is entitled to those damages under the evidence.

IV. RESPONSE TO THE COMPLAINT

A. The Time to Respond
FRCP 12(a) requires that most defendants respond to a complaint within 20 days. The United States government has 60 days to respond, 10 days for motions.

B.   Motions Against the Complaint
The following technicalities can invalidate a complaint and serve the function of alerting the plaintiff or the plaintiff's attorney drafting the complaint to write precisely:

1. Lack of subject matter jurisdiction;

2. Lack of in personam jurisdiction;

3. Improper venue;

4. Insufficiency of process;

5. Insufficiency of service of process;

6. Failure to state a claim upon which relief can be granted; and

7. Failure to join a necessary party.

C.   Motion To Dismiss

1. Background
The motion to dismiss finds its roots in the common-law demurrer. Under the common law, a party could either answer the complaint or demur. If the defendant demurred, and the demurrer was overruled, he was not allowed to contest the facts of the complaint. Moreover, if the demurrer was sustained, the plaintiff had no right to replead or amend the complaint. These austere requirements were later dropped, allowing a defendant to proceed to the merits if the demurrer was overruled and to allow the plaintiff to amend the complaint if the demurrer was sustained.

2. Motion To Dismiss For Failure To State A Claim
The federal system's counterpart to the common-law demurrer is FRCP 12(b)(6), motion to dismiss for failure to state a claim upon which relief can be granted. FRCP-

12(b)(6) must be viewed in light of other rules, such as FRCP 8.

3. Motion For More Definite Statement
   Under FRCP 12(b)(6) a cause of action does not fail if a plaintiff does not set forth the allegations of his complaint with particularity. Instead of moving to dismiss the complaint, the defendant should move for a more definite statement.

4. Motion To Strike
   Under FRCP 12(f) a party may motion to strike his opponent's pleadings when they contain scandalous, impertinent, and irrelevant information. To strike material as scandalous it must be obviously false and unrelated to the subject matter of the action. Even when allegations are not related to the subject matter of the case, in most cases they will not be stricken from a complaint unless their presence will prejudice the adverse party. Prejudice to the adverse party turns on whether the contents of the pleadings will be disclosed to the jury.

5. Motion to Strike the Pleading.
   This motion challenges the entire pleading because it was filed too late, necessary court approval had not been obtained, or other rules of order had not been satisfied.

6. Plaintiff's Response
   If a motion to dismiss under FRCP 12(b)(6) is granted by the court, the plaintiff can choose between two avenues: abandon the action or appeal (i.e., the plaintiff is not "locked-in" if a motion to dismiss is granted and can still appeal).

V.   ANSWERING THE COMPLAINT

A.   Generally
     The answer serves a notice function. The court has to know the defendant's reply to the complaint. Under FRCP 15,

pleadings can be liberally amended. This rule serves as a consideration both to the plaintiff and to the plaintiff's attorney (i.e., if the plaintiff misunderstood some fact and included this error in the pleading or the plaintiff's attorney failed to carefully and thoroughly research a point of law, the plaintiff will not suffer a loss as a result). Therefore, the rules favor a very liberal amendment policy.

B.   Requirements Of An Answer
Under FRCP 8, a defendant must do one of three things to the paragraphs of plaintiff's complaint:

1. Defendant may deny the allegations.

2. Defendant may admit the allegations.

3. Defendant may plead insufficient information in response to each allegation.

C.   Failure To Answer
If defendant fails to specifically respond to an averment, he is deemed to have admitted it. As a safeguard against inadvertent admission, defendants usually add an all-inclusive paragraph denying each and every averment unless otherwise admitted.

D.   General Denials
General denials of the entire complaint are permitted under FRCP 8 and under most state rules. This is very risky. If a court rules that a general denial does not meet the substance of the denied averments, the defendant may be deemed to have admitted the plaintiff's specific averments. Moreover, general denials do not put into issue matters that under FRCP 9 must be specifically challenged.

E.   Affirmative Defenses
FRCP 8(c) enumerates 19 affirmative defenses which must be specifically raised. Generally, defendants are required to raise such affirmative defenses that do not logically flow from

plaintiff's complaint. In deciding whether a defense must be raised affirmatively, courts generally look to statutes in federal questions and to state practice in diversity actions.

VI. THE REPLY

FRCP 7(a) permits a reply to a counterclaim and allows courts to order plaintiff to reply to allegations other than counterclaims. According to FRCP 8(d), allegations to which a reply is neither required nor permitted are considered denied or avoided, and plaintiff may contest them at trial. Under FRCP 8(d) allegations requiring responsive pleadings are deemed admitted if not denied in the reply.

VII. AMENDMENTS

A. Generally

1. Before a Reply
    FRCP 15(a) allows a party to amend its pleading once before a responsive pleading is served, or if no responsive pleading is permitted and the action has not been placed on the trial calendar, 20 days after service.

2. Three-Strike Rule
    A party may otherwise amend its pleading with the written consent of the adverse party or by leave of court, which shall be freely given when justice so requires. Most courts follow an unofficial three-strike rule, which gives a party three chances to correct defects in its pleadings, after which the court will find that justice no longer requires another opportunity. A party must amend a pleading within the response time to the original pleading or 10 days after service of the amended pleading, whichever period may be longer, unless the court orders otherwise.

B.   Amendments to Conform to the Evidence
      FRCP 15(b) states that issues not raised by the pleadings
      when tried by the consent of the parties shall be treated as if
      raised in the pleadings. This motion can be made at anytime,
      even after judgment.

C.   Relating Back Amendments
      FRCP 15(c) states that when a claim or defense asserted in an
      amended pleading arose out of the conduct, transaction, or
      occurrence set forth or attempted to be set forth in the origi-
      nal pleading, the amendment relates back to the date of the
      original pleading for purposes of statutes of limitations.

D.   Supplemental Pleadings (FRCP 15(d))
      Where relevant activity occurs after the pleadings have been
      filed, the court has discretion to allow the parties to file
      supplemental pleadings to reflect the new circumstances.

CASE CLIPS

Scott v. Shepherd (The Squib Case) (1773)
Facts: Scott brought a trespass action when his eye was put out
by a lighted squib made of gunpowder that had originally been
lighted by Shepherd. But in the moments between the lighting and
the explosion, the squib had been thrown about by several others
to avoid injury.
Issue: When is an action in trespass maintainable?
Rule: Two theories are advocated by the four judges: 1) a trespass
action is maintainable if the injury is caused by an illegal act; and
2) a trespass action is maintainable if an injury is the immediate
result of an action. There is difficulty in deciding whether an
injury is "immediate" or "consequential."

Logan v. Southern Cal. Rapid Transit District (1982)

Facts: Following an altercation with a passenger, Logan was fired from his job as a bus driver. He admitted in his pleadings that he was provided with a hearing, but claimed that his due process rights were violated. Apparently, he was not allowed to testify at the hearing or call an important witness. However, he did not allege these facts in his complaint. The defendants demurred on the ground that Logan failed to state a cause of action.

Issue: What facts must be alleged in a complaint in order to state a cause of action?

Rule: To successfully state a cause of action, a complaint must allege ultimate facts, not evidentiary facts or conclusions of law. Here, the defendants' demurrers were sustained because Logan claimed his due process rights were violated, but failed to allege any ultimate facts as to how his due process rights were violated.

Note: This is a California case. Courts that follow the Federal Rules have largely abandoned the evidentiary fact/ultimate fact/conclusion-of-law distinction in favor of more general allegations.

Campbell v. Laurel (1990)

Facts: Campbell alleged that Laurel, her probation officer, informed her that her status as a lawful, complying probationer depended on her willingness to have sex with him. Her complaint alleged violations of a state civil rights act, intentional infliction of emotional distress, gross negligence and violation of 44 U.S.C. § 1983. 42 U.S.C. § 1983 provides a cause of action where conduct committed by a person acting under state law deprives a person of rights, privileges, or immunities secured by the Constitution or laws of the United States. Laurel made a 12(b)(6) motion to dismiss for failure to state a claim.

Issue: What facts must be alleged in a complaint in order to state a cause of action?

Rule: To be sufficient, pleadings must allege enough information to outline the elements of a claim or permit the inference that these elements exist. Conclusory allegations that require courts to conjure up unpleaded facts to support the allegations are not sufficient. The demurrer here was properly sustained because the facts alleged by Campbell only support claims under state law (i.e., tort). She failed to allege facts to support a § 1983 action, such as the acts were a policy or custom of the agency, negligence in training, etc.

Rannels v. S.E. Nichols, Inc. (1979)

Facts: Rannels stopped payment on a check due to a dispute over defective merchandise she purchased from Nichols. Nichols filed a criminal complaint alleging violation of a bad check statute, although it knew why she had stopped payment. Rannels brought the present suit for wrongful prosecution and alleged those facts in her complaint. The district court dismissed the action on grounds that the complaint failed to aver lack of probable cause (an element necessary for a wrongful prosecution claim).

Issue: Under the federal rules, must a complaint allege facts necessary to support every element of a cause of action?

Rule: The federal rules only require that a complaint contain a short, plain statement of the claim to give the defendant fair notice of what the plaintiff's claim is and the grounds on which it rests. Malice, intent, knowledge, and other conditions of mind need not be specifically averred.

Business Guides v. Chromatic Communications Enterprises. (S.Ct. 1991)

Facts: Business Guides published various trade directories. The directories contained "seeds", which were deliberate errors planted to provide evidence of copyright infringement if they turn up in competitors' directories. Business Guides sought a temporary restraining order against Chromatic Communications, alleging that its directory contained ten seeds. A one-hour investigation by a law clerk revealed that nine of the ten were actually legitimate listings. Chromatic Communications sought Rule 11 sanctions against Business Guides and their attorneys, Finley, Kumble. Because Finley, Kumble was in bankruptcy, the motion was only pursued against Chromatic Communications, which was held liable for $13,866.

Issue 1: What is the standard of care imposed by Rule 11?

Rule 1: (O'Connor, J.) Any party who signs a pleading, motion or other paper has an affirmative duty to conduct a reasonable inquiry into the facts and the law before filing. The applicable standard is reasonableness under the circumstances.

Issue 2: To whom does Rule 11 apply?

Rule 2: Rule 11 applies to those whose signatures are present on court papers, whether an attorney or a party, and whether or not their signatures were required.

Dissent: (Kennedy, J.) The purpose of Rule 11 is to control the practice of attorneys or those who act as their own attorneys. It is an abuse of discretion to sanction a represented litigant who acts in good faith but errs as to the facts.

DiLeo v. Ernst & Young (1990)

Facts: DiLeo was an investor in Continental Illinois Bank ["Continental"], which lost four billion dollars. Ernst & Young ["E & Y"] was Continental's accountant. DiLeo brought an action against E & Y for securities fraud. The central allegation of the complaint was that before investors bought their stock, E & W "became aware that a substantial amount of the receivables reported in Continental's financial statement were likely to be uncollectible." They became uncollectible.

Issue: What must a complaint allege in an action for fraud?

Rule: Although states of mind may be pleaded generally, circumstances constituting fraud must be stated with particularity. Here, the plaintiff did not provide any facts to indicate that the change in the stated condition of the firm was even due to negligence, let alone fraud.

Fisher v. Flynn (1979)

Facts: Fisher brought a Title VII sex discrimination suit against Bridgewater State College for her dismissal as an assistant professor. Her only allegation of specific conduct was that "some part" of the reason for her dismissal was that she refused the romantic advances of her department chairman.

Issue: What must a complaint allege in a civil rights action?

Rule: Complaints based on civil rights violations must do more than state simple conclusions; they must at least outline the facts constituting the alleged violation. Fisher did not allege a sufficient nexus between her refusal of the romantic overtures and her termination because she did not allege that the department chairman had the authority to terminate her employment.

Gomez v. Toledo (S.Ct. 1980)

Facts: In a suit under 42 U.S.C. § 1983, Gomez alleged that in dismissing him from the Puerto Rican Police Force, the city of Toledo violated the principles of procedural due process. Gomez neglected to allege that the city had acted in bad faith, although the city was perfectly within its rights to dismiss Gomez in good faith.

Issue: Is it necessary for a plaintiff to allege that an official acted in bad faith to state a claim against a public official under 42 U.S.C. § 1983?

Rule: (Marshall, J.) In an action against a public official whose position may entitle him to immunity if he acted in good faith, a plaintiff need not allege bad faith on the part of the official in order to state a claim for relief under 42 U.S.C. § 1983.

Zielinski v. Philadelphia Piers, Inc. (1956)

Facts: Zielinski was injured in an accident by a forklift driven by Johnson. Philadelphia Piers officers were present at a deposition where Johnson said he worked for Philadelphia Piers. Philadelphia Piers did not respond then, but later denied that it employed Johnson.

Issue: May a defendant knowingly allow a plaintiff to rely on erroneous facts in the complaint?

Rule: A defendant who knowingly makes false statements upon which a plaintiff relies will be estopped from denying such statements at trial.

Layman v. Southwestern Bell Tel. Co. (1977)

Facts: Southwestern Bell ["Bell"] had a subcontractor dig up part of Layman's property. Layman brought a trespass action. Bell's answer contained only a general denial. At trial, Bell sought to introduce evidence that it had an easement across the property (an affirmative defense).

Issue: May a party introduce evidence supporting an affirmative defense when it has only pled a general denial in its answer?

Rule: A defendant is obligated to plead affirmative defenses in its answer. If a defendant only pleads a general denial, it may not offer evidence establishing affirmative defenses.

Beeck v. Aquaslide `N' Dive Corp. (1977)

Facts: Beeck was injured while using a water slide. Aquaslide `N' Dive Corp. initially admitted it was the slide's manufacturer, but later moved to amend its answer to deny manufacturing the slide. The motion was granted.

Issue: When may a court grant a motion to amend an answer?

Rule: A court may grant a motion to amend an answer unless the opposing party can show he would be prejudiced if the motion is granted.

Barnes v. Callaghan & Co. (1977)

Facts: Barnes was fired from her job at Callaghan. She brought suit against Callaghan, alleging sexual discrimination. Barnes amended her complaint to state a claim for slander. The statute of limitations for slander had run by the time the complaint was amended, but had not yet run when the original complaint was filed. Barnes' original complaint did not allege malice or publication, which are elements of a well-pleaded slander action. FRCP 15(c) provided that an amended claim relates back to the date of the original pleading if it arose out of the conduct, transaction, or occurrence set forth in the original pleading.

Issue: What are the requirements for an amended claim to relate back to the original complaint?

Rule: An amended complaint relates back to the original pleadings if the original pleadings contained timely, specific allegations of the conduct or transaction on which the amended claim is based such that the defendant has adequate notice of the action. Because Barnes' original complaint only alleged facts that stated Title VII and breech of contract claims, the slander claim was regarded as a new cause of action (which was consequently time-barred).

Chapter 6

JOINDER

I. ABILITY TO SUE

A. Justiciability

1. The Supreme Court and lower federal courts will only hear justiciable cases, i.e., cases appropriate for federal adjudication on the merits.

2. Sources of Justiciability Standards
   The conditions necessary for justiciability are derived either from interpretations of the Article III, § 2 requirement that there be a "case or controversy," or from general Supreme Court policies developed apart from the Constitution.

3. Requirements for Justiciability
   A suit is justiciable when certain conditions are present.

   Mnemonic: **SCRiMPS**

   a. **S**tanding
      A plaintiff must have standing to invoke the adjudicatory power of the federal courts. Standing is created when the plaintiff has a personal stake in the suit's outcome. The "personal stake" requirement is met where:

      i. There is distinct and palpable (not speculative) injury to the plaintiff;

      ii. A fairly traceable causal connection exists between the claimed injury and the challenged conduct; and

      iii. There is a substantial likelihood that the relief requested will prevent or redress the claimed injury.

iv. Taxpayer Standing
A taxpayer will have standing to challenge a Congressional expenditure only if it meets the dual-nexus test established in *Flast v. Cohen*.

(1) The expenditure must be an exercise of power under the Taxing and Spending Clause.

(2) The expenditure must violate a specific constitutional provision that limits the taxing and spending power, such as the prohibition against an established religion. In reviewing a suit that requests more than one type of relief, the Supreme Court will impose a separate standing test for each.

b. Case or Controversy
The issues must arise out of an actual and current case or controversy between adverse litigants. Adjudication of hypothetical or removed disputes would result in advisory opinions — something federal courts may not issue.

c. Ripeness
The case must be ripe for review, i.e., the issues must be fully crystallized and the controversy concrete. Ripeness is established when litigants claim actual interference with their rights. Hypothetical threats to those rights do not invoke federal adjudicatory power.

d. Mootness (*DeFunis v. Odegaard*)
A federal case must involve controversies that are active and ongoing at the time of adjudication. A case becomes moot, and thus ineligible for judgment on the merits, once the controversy between the parties ceases to be definite and concrete and when a court's decision would no longer affect the litigants' rights.

e. Political Questions
A suit is nonjusticiable as a political question if:

   i.   The issues involve resolution of questions commit-
        ted by the Constitution's text to a coordinate gov-
        ernmental branch;

   ii. There is a lack of judicially discoverable and man-
        ageable standards for resolving the case, or if a
        decision would require a policy determination
        clearly outside judicial discretion; and

   iii. Judicial intervention would produce an embarrass-
        ing diversity of pronouncements on the issue by
        various governmental departments.

f. Self-restraint/Discretion
There must not be a risk that federal adjudication
would breach principles of judicial self-restraint and
discretion. For example, federal courts and the Supreme Court avoid suits that would entail interfering
with:

   i.   State courts' ability to resolve federal question cases;

   ii. Pending state court proceedings; or

   iii. Execution of state court judgments.
        Judicial self-restraint recognizes the importance of
        preserving the balance between state and federal
        interests. Such restraint also prevents the unwarrant-
        ed federal constitutional decisions that may result
        when federal courts interpret state statutes.

4. The Problem of "Jus Tertii"
The Supreme Court and lower federal courts will not
recognize the standing of a plaintiff who represents the
constitutional rights of third parties ("jus tertii"), i.e., those

not parties to the case. This rule is not constitutionally based; it is founded on policies of judicial self-restraint.

    a. The Court hesitates to permit assertions of "jus tertii" (third-party rights) because:

        i. Nonparties may not want to assert their own rights;

        ii. Nonparty rights may be unaffected by the litigation's outcome; and

        iii. Third parties are often the best proponents of their own interests.

    b. Federal courts may recognize "jus tertii" standing when:

        i. The nonparties' rights are inextricably bound up with the activity the litigant wishes to pursue;

        ii. The plaintiff is no less effective a proponent of third party rights than the third parties themselves; and

        iii. There is a genuine obstacle to the nonparties' representing their own interests.

B.   Real Party in Interest (FRCP 17(a))

    1. Defined
    Every action shall be prosecuted in the name of the real party in interest (RPI). The RPI is the individual or individuals who will be directly affected by the action at hand.

    2. Insurers
    An insurer that has fully paid a claim to an insured individual would be the RPI in any action to recover damages, since the insured has already been compensated.

Had the claim been only partially paid, however, both the insured and the insurer could be real parties in interest.

C.   Capacity to Sue and Be Sued (FRCP 17(b))

1. Defined
States sometimes condition some groups' ability to enforce rights and obligations. For instance, minors and mental incompetents often cannot sue or be sued, except in specific cases.

2. Individuals
The ability of an individual to enforce rights or duties against others is determined by the state in which the person is domiciled.

3. Corporations
A corporation's capacity to sue or be sued is determined by the law of the state under which the corporation is incorporated.

4. Unincorporated Associations
Even if state law does not grant unincorporated associations the capacity to sue or be sued, FRCP 17 grants such capacity to these groups where federal or constitutional rights or obligations are at stake.

II.   JOINDER OF CLAIMS

A.   Generally (FRCP 18)
A party may join several causes of action as long as they arise out of the same transaction or occurrence, or series of transactions or occurrences. This transactional test applies whether the second claim is brought by a plaintiff against a defendant, by a defendant against a plaintiff (counterclaim), or by one party against a coparty (cross-claim).

B.   Counterclaims (FRCP 13)
      Defendant asserts a claim against a plaintiff. If the defendant's claim is not transactionally related to the claim asserted by the plaintiff, the judge has the discretion to refuse the joinder to avoid unduly complicating the case.

C.   Compulsory Counterclaims (FRCP 13(a))
      Some jurisdictions require all transactionally related counterclaims to be brought by the defendant. A compulsory counterclaim that has not been asserted cannot be raised in a subsequent lawsuit in federal court and compulsory counterclaim jurisdictions.

D.   Cross-Claims (FRCP 13(g))
      Parties to a lawsuit (either plaintiffs or defendants) can assert crossclaims against their coparties (coplaintiffs or codefendants, respectively) if the claims arise out of the same transaction as the case at hand.

III. JOINDER OF PARTIES

A.   Permissive Joinder (FRCP 20)
      Outside parties to an action may consent to be joined by leave of the court. The joined parties must have claims that are transactionally related to the original action.

B.   Necessary Parties (FRCP 19(a))

      1. Generally
         Necessary parties to an action must be joined if possible, but their nonjoinder will not result in dismissal. A court will deem a party to be necessary if:

         a. The party's absence will preclude complete relief to present parties;

         b. The party's absence will preclude complete relief to that party in a subsequent suit; or

    c. The party's absence may subject a present party to multiple liability.

 2. Involuntary Necessary Party

A necessary party who does not consent to joinder may be made a defendant or an involuntary third-party plaintiff upon order of the court. However, if the court does not have proper jurisdiction over the party, or if venue is improper, the court may continue the action without this "necessary" party.

C. Indispensable Parties (FRCP 19(b))

 1. Generally

Indispensable parties are those whose presence at trial is so necessary that their joinder will be compelled, even at the cost of dismissing the action, if that party cannot be joined.

 2. Factors

A court may deem a necessary party to be indispensable by weighing how that party's absence will affect the following factors:

    a. Prejudice to parties present as well as the necessary party;

    b. Judicial options that may alleviate that prejudice;

    c. Adequacy of the judgment without the party; and

    d. Alternative remedies for the plaintiff in case of dismissal.

D. Consolidation (FRCP 42)

1. Consolidating Cases
    Where several transactionally related actions are before the same court, the judge may order all of those actions to be consolidated in one suit.

2. Policy
    Combined discovery, shared costs, and general reduction in delay.

3. Separation
    Alternatively, where consolidation actually hinders speedy adjudication of the suits, the judge may also order separation.

4. Multidistrict Litigation (28 U.S.C. § 1407)
    Transactionally related claims occurring in separate federal courts may be consolidated for concurrent discovery and other pretrial procedures upon a proper determination by a judicial panel on multidistrict litigation. This measure has been used frequently with asbestos liability and other mass tort litigation.

E. Impleader (FRCP 22)

1. Generally
    Impleader is a device by which the defendant joins a third party to a suit under the theory that if the defendant is liable to the plaintiff, then this third party is also at least partially responsible.

2. Policy

    a. Judicial efficiency

    b. Prevent multiple liability, or windfall decisions
        Prevents a plaintiff from first suing the defendant and then the third party, recovering twice from both.

3. Jurisdiction
The impleaded party must have independent subject matter jurisdiction regarding the plaintiff, and cannot destroy diversity jurisdiction.

F. Intervention (FRCP 24)

1. Generally
Intervention allows a third party to join an action, even if neither the plaintiffs nor the defendants request that party's presence. The intervenor may present both new claims and defenses to charges.

2. Permissive Intervention (FRCP 24(b))
Courts have the discretion to allow a petitioner to intervene if either:

a. A federal statute confers such a right to intervene; or

b. The petitioner's claim or defense is transactionally related to the main action.

3. Intervention as of Right
The court must allow a petitioner to intervene if either:

a. A federal statute confers such an absolute right; or

b. The petitioner presents:

i. A transactionally related claim or defense;

ii. Without adjudication, the petitioner's rights would be impaired or impeded; and

iii. Existing parties would not adequately represent the petitioner's interests.

c. Courts will generally use the same analysis in determining whether a petitioner may intervene as of right as it does when determining whether a party is indispensable under FRCP 19.

G. Interpleader

1. Generally
    Interpleader allows one party to join various adverse claimants who each have separate claims to a single piece of property or fund, where that property cannot be split among the adverse claimants to the satisfaction of all the claims. This procedure is used most often by insurance companies who must pay out a limited fund to several parties.

2. Rule Interpleader (FRCP 22)
    As long as general jurisdictional requirements are met, and none of the interpleaded parties ruin the requirement of complete diversity, FRCP 22 allows the debtor to join all the parties. Diversity in this context means that none of the claimants may be from the same state as the debtor.

3. Statutory Interpleader (28 U.S.C. § 1335)
    Since most interpleaders will not satisfy the traditional elements of diversity jurisdiction, Congress enacted a second interpleader statute. This statute differs from rule interpleader in several respects.

    a. The amount in controversy need be only $500, as opposed to the $50,000 normally required for diversity jurisdiction.

    b. Minimum, not complete diversity is required. So long as any two claimants are diverse regarding one another, diversity is satisfied.

    c. The property being disputed must be deposited with the court throughout the proceedings.

IV.   CLASS ACTIONS

A.   Defined
Class actions are lawsuits brought (or defended) by several representative members on behalf of all group members, pursuant to FRCP 23.

B.   Jurisdiction
The class representative must satisfy the requirements of subject matter jurisdiction, personal jurisdiction, and venue.

V.   PREREQUISITES (FRCP 23(a))

A.   Policy
Before certifying a class, the judge must determine that certain prerequisites have been met. The prerequisites for a class action mandate the principle that one cannot automatically file a class action unless there is a definable class with specific interests at issue in the controversy.

B.   Elements
FRCP 23(a) requires that four conditions be satisfied before there is any possibility of a class action:

Mnemonic: **CAN'T**

1. Commonality
    The class must present common questions of law and fact.

2. Adequacy
    The representatives must fairly and adequately represent the interests of the class.

3. Numerosity
    The size of the class must be very large so that joinder is not possible (i.e., people are from different jurisdictions or cannot afford to join).

4. Typicality
The representatives must present claims and defenses typical of those of the class.

VI.   NAMED REPRESENTATIVE

A.   Policy
After certifying the class, the court will seek out an individual who will represent that class. Every class of litigants is represented by what is known as a named plaintiff. This is generally the individual who initially files the class action.

B.   Elements

1. Satisfy Requirements
Named representatives must satisfy the four requirements pursuant to FRCP 23.

2. Common Injury
Named representatives filing a class action must show a common injury.

3. Common Claims
Named representatives must be suing on similar legal grounds.

C.   Headless Class Actions
In cases of class action defendants, or where the original class action plaintiff withdraws from the litigation or is disqualified, there may be a situation where a valid class action exists without a named representative. These are so-called headless class actions. A court then has several options:

1. Voluntary Replacement
The court may allow the attorneys for a disqualified named representative to locate a new individual, who fulfills all of the qualifications for named representative,

to voluntarily pick up where the disqualified representative left off.

2. Assigned Representative
For class action defendants, and some class action plaintiffs, a court may simply assign a named representative to prevent dismissal of an action.

3. Retained Representative
The court may decide to maintain the original named representative despite a technical disqualification, such as mootness (as regarding the individual named plaintiff). But the court must be sure that the named individual will proceed in the best interests of the class.

VII. CERTIFICATION

A. Policy
Having certified the class and located a named representative, a judge must then decide what type of class action will proceed. FRCP 23(b) sets out three types of class actions. These classifications are not mutually exclusive, and a single class action may be certified under more than one classification. Furthermore, some issues may be certified under one classification, while other issues in the same class action may be certified under others.

B. Types of Class Actions

1. Legal Class Action (FRCP 23(b)(1))
The most common type of class action occurs if either of two criteria are present:

a. Inconsistent Results
Often there is a danger that, if litigated separately, severe injustice could accrue to one or more of the class members. Examples are where substantive rights are at issue that might determine future conduct (e.g., patent infringement); or

b. Dispositive Adjudication
Occasionally, one litigation could effectively litigate a claim of a party not present. For instance in mass tort litigation, were suits to be brought individually a defendant may go bankrupt paying out large claims (or simply by defending individual suits) to the first few plaintiffs, before others, who may be even more seriously injured, get a chance to even litigate. This class action would allow all injured parties to at least get partial adjudication.

2. Injunctive Relief (FRCP 23(b)(2))
Class actions will be certified under FRCP 23(b)(2) where the court has properly certified the class and has determined that injunctive or declaratory relief may be necessary.

3. Predominating Issues of Law or Fact (FRCP 23(b)(3))
That individual class members are not identical with regard to the claims against the common defendant (or defenses against a common plaintiff) will not preclude certification if some issues of law or fact, common to all class members, predominate. A court will look at the following factors:

Mnemonic: **COIL**

a. **C**oncentration
Desirability of concentrating litigation in one forum, where the class members may be from many different jurisdictions, and subject to different laws.

b. **O**versight
Difficulties in managing a class action with many different claims and parties who may have different interests.

c. **I**ndividual Control

Interest of individuals in controlling their own suits, as opposed to being thrown into a class-driven suit, where their individual concerns may not be as adequately addressed.

d. Litigation
Extent of litigation already started by other class members that may be impeded by the onset of a class action.

C.   Conditional Certification (FRCP 23(c)(1))
A certification order may be made conditional, or altered or amended to reflect a change in circumstances (i.e., a court determines a certain subclass should be decertified, or the class should be expanded, or the case requires injunctive relief, etc.)

VIII. NOTICE

A.   Policy
It is not normally possible to individually notify all the class members because they are too numerous, or because not all the members can be positively identified. FRCP 23(c)(2) and 23(c)(3) require different notice depending on the type of class action certified.

B.   Requirements for FRCP 23(b)(3) Class Actions (FRCP 23(c)(2))

1. Best Notice Practicable
The court must notify FRCP 23(b)(3) class members in the best practicable way. The Supreme Court has held that this means that every class member must receive individual notice.

2. Opt-Out Provisions
Notice to FRCP 23(b)(3) members must include notification that individuals may be able to "opt out" of the class. If they opt out, an adverse judgment will not be binding on them, but neither will they receive any benefit of a

favorable judgment. If they neglect to opt out (even if they do not actively opt in) any judgment will be binding, whether they participate actively or not.

C. Requirements for FRCP 23(b)(1) and 23(b)(2) Class Actions (FRCP 23(c)(3))

   1. Judicial Discretion
     Courts have wide discretion in notifying class members under FRCP 23(b)(1) and 23(b)(2). This may include individual notice, or notice by publication. Some courts have gone so far as to require the named representative to take out large newspaper, magazine and television advertising to contact as many potential class members as possible.

   2. No Opt-Out
     Individual class members may not opt out of FRCP 23-(b)(1) and 23(b)(2) class actions. That is why notice requirements are not as stringent. However, this means that a class member may become bound by a suit to which the member neither had notice nor input.

D. Costs of Notice
   Often, the named representative must bear the cost of notice. However, if the individual defendant (or plaintiff) can afford to notify the class members less expensively, a court may require that defendant to notify all class members, with a reimbursement by the named representative if the costs are substantial.

IX. JUDGMENTS

A. Preclusive Effect
   Class actions have the same preclusive effect in all class members as any other suit may have. (See Chapter 11) A judgment in a class action is binding on all members of the class unless there is an opportunity to opt out of the class and the class member takes advantage of that opportunity.

B. Attorney's Fees
    The court's award of attorney's fees is separate from the plaintiff's award. This is unusual because in most cases attorney's fees are paid by the plaintiff out of whatever award is granted (if any).

C. Settlements (FRCP 23(e))
    Class actions may be settled by agreement between the named representative and the individual defendant (or plaintiff), as long as:

    1. Notice is provided to members of the class, and

    2. The settlement is approved by the court.

CASE CLIPS

Plant v. Blazer Financial Services (1979)

Facts: Plant executed a note in favor of Blazer. Plant brought suit under the federal Truth in Lending Act for failure to make required disclosures. The defendant brought a counterclaim on the underlying debt. There was no independent jurisdictional basis for the federal court to adjudicate the counterclaim (i.e., federal question or diversity jurisdiction), such that the court could only hear the counterclaim if it was compulsory.

Issue: When is a counterclaim compulsory?

Rule: A counterclaim is compulsory when there is a logical relationship between the claim and the counterclaim that indicates that they arose from the same aggregate of operative facts. Because both actions in this suit arose from a single loan transaction and depend on overlapping evidence, the court held that the action on the underlying debt was a compulsory counterclaim to the truth-in-lending action.

Mosley v. General Motors Corp. (1974)

Facts: Mosley and nine others jointly filed suit alleging that General Motors and their union discriminated against them on the basis of race and/or sex. FRCP 20(a) provided that all persons may join in one action as plaintiffs if they assert any right to relief arising out of the same transaction(s) and if any questions of law or fact are common to all. The district court severed the action, having found that there were a variety of issues having little relationship to each other beyond a common defendant.

Issue: Does a Title VII action brought by several plaintiffs who allege discrimination by a common employer satisfy the FRCP 20(a) joinder requirements?

Rule: Parties may join as plaintiffs in a suit brought on the basis of a company-wide policy of discrimination because it arises out of the same series of transactions and depends on similar questions of law and fact, even if the actual effects of the policy (i.e., damages) vary throughout the class.

Watergate Landmark Condo Unit
Owners Ass'n v. Wiss, Janey, Elstner Assoc. (1987)

Facts: The plaintiffs employed Legum & Norman to manage their condominiums. Legum and Norman hired the defendant, an engineering firm, to draw plans to repair crumbling balconies. Based on the defendant's plans, the plaintiff employed Brisk Waterproofing to repair the balconies. The plaintiff sued Legum & Norman (the managers) and the defendant engineers because they were not satisfied with the repairs. The complaint conceded that Brisk's work was performed properly. Legum & Norman filed a third party complaint against Brisk Waterproofing.

Issue: When is a third party complaint proper?

Rule: A third party claim is only appropriate if the third party plaintiff is claiming that the third party defendant is derivatively liable to him (i.e., the third party defendant must reimburse the original defendant for all or part of anything he must pay the original plaintiff). It is not appropriate in suits such as this, where the defendant makes a third party claim in order to state, "It was him, not me."

Owen Equipment & Erection Co. v. Kroger
(S.Ct. 1978)

Facts: Kroger brought a wrongful death action in federal court, based on diversity of citizenship. The original defendant impleaded Owen Equipment and Erection Co. as a third-party defendant. The original defendant was granted summary judgment, leaving Owen as the sole defendant. It was subsequently discovered that Kroger and Owen were citizens of the same state.

Issue: In an action in which federal jurisdiction rests solely on diversity of citizenship, may the court exercise ancillary jurisdiction under FRCP 14, of a claim against an impleaded third-party defendant whose citizenship is the same as the plaintiff's?

Rule: (Stewart, J.) Title 28 U.S.C. § 1332(a)(1) requires complete diversity of citizenship. The federal court in a diversity case may therefore not assume ancillary jurisdiction under FRCP 14 of an action against a third-party defendant whose citizenship is identical with the plaintiff's.

Dissent: (White, J.) Since Kroger's claims against Owen and OPPD arose from a common nucleus of operative facts, the federal court should be able to hear the claim against Owen, following the Court's previous holding in *Mine Workers v. Gibbs*. This Court reads the diversity jurisdiction statute too narrowly.

Amco Constr. Co. v. Mississippi State Bldg Comm'n (1979)

Facts: Mississippi State Building Commission ["Commission"] hired Amco to construct a park. Amco posted a performance and payment bond, using Houston General as surety. Amco also hired subcontractors. Amco subsequently abandoned the project. A subcontractor sued Houston General in federal diversity jurisdiction for payment on the bond. Houston General filed third party claims against Amco and Commission for indemnification. Amco then filed a cross-claim against Commission, claiming that Commission furnished defective plans and specifications. There was no diversity between Amco and Commission.

Issue: When is it proper for a federal court to extend ancillary jurisdiction to a cross-claim that has no independent basis of jurisdiction?

Rule: A claim is ancillary if it arises out of the same aggregate of operative facts as an original claim over which the court has jurisdiction. The claim arises out of the same facts if the same facts serve as the basis of both claims or the facts upon which the original claim rests activates additional previously dormant legal rights in a defendant. In the instant case, the original suit was for performance on a bond, whereas the cross claim was for breach of contract. The claims arose from different transactions, required substantially distinct fact-finding efforts, and the cross-claim did not depend on the original claim for its existence. Therefore, supplemental jurisdiction did not extend to the cross-claim.

Helzberg's Diamond Shops v. Valley West Des Moines Shopping Center (1977)

Facts: Helzberg entered into a lease agreement with Valley West that provided that Valley West would not lease space to more than two additional jewelry stores. Valley West leased space to a third jewelry store, Lord's. Helzberg sued Valley West, seeking injunctive relief. Lord could not be joined as a party to the action because it was not subject to personal jurisdiction. Valley West moved to dismiss, for failure to join an indispensable party.

Issue: When should a suit be dismissed for failure to join an indispensable party?

Rule: A suit should be dismissed for failure to join an indispensable party if a judgment rendered in the party's absence would be prejudicial to that party or another defendant. A party is not indispensable to an action to determine rights under a contract simply because that party's rights or obligations under an entirely separate contract will be affected by the result.

Natural Resources Defense Council v. United States Nuclear Regulatory Comm'n (1978)

Facts: The Natural Resources Defense Council sought an injunction to prevent the U.S. Nuclear Regulatory Commission and the New Mexico Environmental Improvement Agency from issuing licenses to uranium mills without first preparing environmental impact statements. Kerr-McGee, a potential license recipient, moved to intervene in the suit, pursuant to FRCP 24. The trial court denied the motion on the ground that the movants interests were well represented by other parties. FRCP 24(a)(2) provided that one can intervene in an action if he has an *interest* relating to the subject of the action and is so situated that the disposition of the action may *impair* his ability to protect that interest, unless the interest is *adequately represented* by existing parties.

Issue: When does a party have a sufficient interest in an action to intervene under FRCP 24(a)(2)?

Rule: A party has a sufficient interest in an action when there is a genuine threat to a substantial degree. A general interest in the public welfare is not a sufficient interest. Any significant legal effect in the applicant's interest satisfies the impairment requirement. The interest is not adequately protected by existing parties if there is even a small possibility that their interests will diverge. The court consequently granted Kerr-McGee's motion.

State Farm Fire & Cas. Co. v. Tashire
(S.Ct. 1967)

Facts: State Farm sought to interplead all prospective claimants involved in a multivehicle accident. The insurance proceeds would not cover the amount of the claims that had already been filed.

Issue: Is a federal interpleader action appropriate before claims have been adjudicated?

Rule: (Fortas, J.) Insurance companies can interplead prospective claimants prior to judgment being rendered. However, a plaintiff may not use interpleader to enjoin prospective claimants from bringing suits outside the jurisdiction of the interpleader action.

Martin v. Wilkes (S.Ct. 1989)

Facts: In the first suit, the National Association for the Advancement of Colored People (NAACP) and seven black firefighters received a publicly announced decree setting forth remedial schemes for the hiring of black people as firefighters. Seven white firefighters sought an injunction to intervene, but were denied relief due to the late filing of their petition to intervene. In the second suit, another group of white firefighters brought suit alleging injury due to enforcement of the decree.

Issue: When are people who are neither a party nor in privity to a party in a suit, prohibited from contesting a judgment?

Rule: (Rehnquist, C.J.) Parties are not bound by previous litigation unless they are joined. There is no duty to intervene in the lawsuit, even if they know their rights may be affected.

Hansberry v. Lee (S.Ct. 1940)

Facts: Hansberry, a black man, purchased land that may have been subject to a racially restrictive covenant. Lee, an owner of land subject to the same covenant, sought to enforce the restriction. According to the covenant, the restriction would only be valid if signed by ninety-five percent of the landowners. In a prior case, to which neither Hansberry nor any other minorities were a party, a state judge had found that ninety-five percent of the landowners had signed.

Issue: Can an individual be bound by a prior action in which he was not a party based on the fact that both he and the party in the previous suit are members of the same class?

Rule: (Stone, J.) Due process requires that members of a class not present as parties to an action be bound by the judgment only if they were adequately represented by the parties present. Such members are also bound if they participate in the litigation, if they have joint interests, or if a legal relationship exists between the parties present and those absent such as to entitle the former to stand in judgment for the latter. None of these criteria was present in this case.

In Re Northern District of California, Dalkon Shield IUD Products Liability Litigation (1982)

Facts: Injured purchasers of Dalkon Shields IUD devices, as well as the manufacturer appealed a district court order conditionally certifying the more than 166 pending suits in the court's district, and thousands of cases throughout the country as both a nationwide class action on the issue of punitive damages and a statewide class action on the issue of liability. Only one plaintiff and no defendants supported the class action measure. The court asserted jurisdiction pursuant to the federal interpleader statute of minimum diversity, holding that since the aggregate claims exceed the net worth of the company, the company itself is a limited fund subject to interpleader.

Issue: May a court compel class certification over the objections of both the plaintiffs and the defendants?

Rule: A court should not certify a statewide class if individual issues outnumber common issues, if the court cannot adequately fulfill the "typical plaintiff" requirement because of differing state standards, and if a class action is not superior to individual actions.

Eisen v. Carlisle & Jacquelin (S.Ct. 1974)

Facts: Eisen filed an antitrust and securities class action. The trial court determined that of the six million members in the class, only 7000 members would be notified personally of the lawsuit. Notice to the other class members would be accomplished by publication. The cost of notice would be distributed between both plaintiffs and defendants after a hearing on the merits.

Issue 1: Is publication sufficient notice for known members of a large class on grounds that personal notice would be too costly?

Rule 1: (Powell, J.) Due process requires that notice be made in the best method possible under the circumstances, including individual notice to all known members.

Issue 2: Can a court hold a preliminary hearing on the merits in order to determine who should pay for notice?

Rule 2: A preliminary hearing on the merits of a class action may prejudice the defendant. The plaintiff must therefore bear the cost of notice to the class except where a fiduciary duty preexisted between plaintiff and defendant.

Phillips Petroleum Co. v. Shutts (S.Ct. 1985)

Facts: Shutts brought a class action suit in Kansas state court on behalf of royalty owners possessing rights to leases with Phillips Petroleum. The members of the class resided throughout the world. Almost all of the leases and class members had no connection with Kansas.

Issue: Can a class action suit be brought in state court though most members of the suit do not have any "minimum contacts" with the forum state?

Rule: (Rehnquist, J.) A forum state may exercise jurisdiction over the claim of an absent class-action plaintiff who lacks "minimum contacts" with the forum. However, the court must provide minimal due process protections, including reasonable notice, opportunity to be heard as well as participate in the litigation, an "opt out" provision, and adequate representation.

Chapter 7

DISCOVERY

Discovery is the obtaining of information prior to trial from opponents and witnesses regarding matters that are relevant to the cause of action.

I.   POLICIES

A.   Goals

    1. Preserve evidence when a witness will not be available for trial.

    2. Narrow the issues that will be introduced at trial.

    3. Control the course of the trial and prevent trial delays and surprises.

    4. Promote just and informed settlements.

B.   Concerns

    1. Control costs of discovery

    2. Prevent use of discovery as a method of one party imposing unreasonable costs on another.

    3. Prevent discovery as a method of harassing the other party.

    4. Prevent parties from gaining evidence through the hard work of others.

II.   SCOPE OF DISCOVERY

A.   Relevancy
The information must be reasonably calculated to lead to the discovery of admissible evidence.

    1. Discovery may not be used as a "fishing expedition."

    2. Discovery may not be used to determine an adversary's legal analysis or strategy.

    3. Nonparties may not be deposed more than 100 miles from where they live. FRCP 45(d)(2).

    4. Depositions may not be used against a party without notice of the deposition. FRCP 32(a).

B.   Discovery Scope and Limits (FRCP 26(b))

    1. Court Discretion (FRCP 26(b)(1))
    Court may limit discovery if:

        a. It is unreasonably duplicative and cumulative;

        b. The information is more easily obtainable elsewhere; or

        c. The discovery request is unduly burdensome.

    2. Insurance Agreements (FRCP 26(b)(2))
    Insurance agreements are always discoverable.

    3. Materials Used in Trial Preparation (FRCP 26(b)(3))
    Only discoverable if there is a substantial need and the party cannot, without undue hardship, obtain the information or equivalent by other means.

4. Experts (FRCP 26(b)(4))

   a. Experts Who Will Testify at Trial (FRCP 26(b)(4)(A))
      Through interrogatories, a party may discover the name, subject matter, summary of facts and opinions, and grounds for each opinion.

      For further discovery, a court order is needed and the discovering party is responsible for costs. FRCP 26(b)(4)(C).

   b. Experts Retained By Counsel But Will Not Testify
      No discovery unless it is impracticable to get the information by other means. There is no discovery of experts consulted but not retained. FRCP 26(b)(4)(B).

   c. Fees
      The discovering party must pay experts a reasonable fee. FRCP 26(b)(4)(A)(ii).

C. Protective Orders (FRCP 26(c))
   The court may prevent or restrict discovery to protect a party from annoyance. The court can also tailor discovery to prevent prejudice.

   1. Purpose
      To protect the privacy of parties and to limit abuses of the discovery process.

   2. Good Cause
      The party requesting protection must show good cause.

   3. Discretion
      Courts have broad discretion in protecting a party from annoyance, embarrassment, oppression or undue burden or expense.

4. General uses

a. Trade Secrets

b. Privileged Information

D. Sequence and Timing of Discovery (FRCP 26(d))
A court may order discovery in a certain order at its discretion.

E. Supplementation of Responses (FRCP 26(e))
Normally not required, with the following exceptions:

1. Questions Addressing:

a. The identity and location of persons; or

b. The identity of experts expected to be called at trial, subject matter of testimony and substance of testimony.

2. New Information

a. Party knows information given is incorrect; or

b. Information given, though true at the time, is no longer true.

F. Verifications and Sanctions (FRCP 26(g))

1. Documentation must be signed by an attorney or an unrepresented party.

2. There must be a good faith belief after reasonable inquiry that information:

a. Is consistent with the rules and warranted by existing law or a good faith extension, modification or reversal of the law;

    b. Is not interposed for an improper purpose such as harassment or delay; and

  3. Is not unduly burdensome or costly given the stakes.

G.   Privilege
Unless the privilege is waived, privileged matters are not discoverable. Examples include information involving:

  1. The lawyer-client relationship.

  2. The doctor-patient relationship.

  3. Husband-wife (i.e., marital confidences).
Some jurisdictions limit the knowledge protected to that gained after the wedding, some jurisdictions protect only information gained before divorce, some protect only information between those two points, and some jurisdictions may not have it at all.

  4. Self-incrimination.

  5. Priest-penitent.

H.   The Work-Product Doctrine (FRCP 26(b)(3),(4))
Information obtained by an attorney while preparing for litigation is not discoverable.

  1. Examples include:

    a. Mental impressions

    b. Conclusions

    c. Opinions

    d. Legal theories

2. Purpose
To promote full investigation of a case.

3. Exceptions

    a. Any party can obtain his or her own statement.

    b. The doctrine cannot be used to hide evidence or to severely prejudice a party.

III.   MECHANICS OF DISCOVERY

A.   Requests to Perpetuate Testimony (FRCP 27)

1. Before Action (FRCP 27(a))
A court order allows parties to depose for the purpose of perpetuating testimony, in preparation for a yet unfiled suit. The potential adverse parties must be named, and the subject matter of the deposition must be disclosed.

2. Pending Appeal (FRCP 27(b))
Such court orders are infrequent, and good cause must first be shown.

B.   Authorization (FRCP 28)
All depositions must take place before a person authorized by the government to take depositions.

C.   Oral Depositions (FRCP 30)

1. Once an action has been filed, no court order is required.

2. A deposition is initiated through the use of a subpoena.

3. Purposes

    a. See how a witness will behave in court under pressure.

    b. Freeze testimony so witness will not recant.

4. Timing (FRCP 30(a))
   A deposition may be taken within thirty days of service of summons and complaint upon a defendant or service made under FRCP 4(e), unless:

   a. Defendant seeks own discovery; or

   b. Witness will abscond the jurisdiction.

5. Corporation as Party (FRCP 30(b)(6))
   The corporation will supply appropriate experts, so that the expert is considered a party whose deposition may be used in the witness' absence.

6. Motion to Limit (FRCP 30(d))
   Depositions will be limited or terminated if they were conducted in bad faith or in a manner calculated to harass the deponent or party.

7. No Show (FRCP 30(g))

   a. Nonparty
      If a nonparty does not show and was not subpoenaed, the deposing party bears the costs.

   b. Party
      If a party does not show, a motion may be made to compel compliance and no subpoena is necessary.

8. Request for Documents (FRCP 30(b)(5))
   The deposing party may attach a request for documents pursuant to FRCP 34 to the notice of deposition. If the deponent is a nonparty the request must take the form of a subpoena duces tecum.

D. Written Depositions (FRCP 31)

   1. No court order is needed.

2. Questions and answers are in written form only.

3. Cheaper method but less useful since there is little flexibility, and the answers will be written by nit-picky literal-minded lawyers.

E.   Interrogatories (FRCP 33)

    1. Parties Only (FRCP 33(a))
Written questions under oath with 30 days to answer.

    2. Documents (FRCP 33(c))
Businesses may provide documents as an answer, but only if the burden is the same for the deponent or the deposing parties to find the answer within the documents.

    3. Goals

        a. Allocate costs based on the knowledge the parties have and their available resources.

        b. The deposing party must do the research.

        c. Prevent the deponent from doing the deposing party's math and statistical analysis.

    4. Concerns

        a. Answers are not generally candid.

        b. Lawyers, and not the party, generally draft the answers.

F.   Requests for Evidence (FRCP 34)
Parties may request production of documents or the right to inspect another party's land or premises if the request is reasonable.

1. Enforceability (FRCP 34(c))
   A separate action may be brought to enforce this order.

2. Class Actions
   This order may even be enforced against class action plaintiffs, even if they are not the named representatives.

G. Physical and Mental Examinations (FRCP 35)

   1. Only enforceable against parties.

   2. Court will try to protect the person's privacy as much as possible.

      a. The health of the party must be in controversy.

      b. The scope of the examination must be specifically stated.

      c. Court order is required and will only be granted if good cause is shown.

   3. Failure to comply will bring sanctions, but generally not contempt.

   4. The party examined may generally not see the report unless the party waives all doctor/patient privileges, so both sides will get each other's medical reports.

H. Requests for Admissions (FRCP 36)

   1. A party may request another to admit a matter presently at issue.

   2. The failure to admit or deny an issue is an admission.

   3. If a party denies an issue that has already been proven, forcing the other party to reprove it at trial, sanctions may be imposed. FRCP 37(c).

4. An admission may be retracted at the court's discretion.

I.   Nonparty Documents (FRCP 45(b))
Are only accessible if a court issues a subpoena duces tecum.

IV.   SANCTIONS FOR NONCOMPLIANCE (FRCP 37)

A.   Motions To Compel Discovery
The refusing party must pay reasonable expenses incurred in obtaining a court order if refusal was without sufficient justification.

B.   Failure to Comply with Court Order

1. Opposing party can be held in contempt of court.

2. Failure to respond to requests could be deemed admission of the facts.

3. Opposing party can be fined or imprisoned.

4. An action or defense can be dismissed.

CASE CLIPS

Blank v. Sullivan & Cromwell (1976)

Facts: A group of female lawyers were rejected for associate positions at Sullivan & Cromwell. As part of a Title VII action, they sought to discover information regarding the defendant's partner selections. Under FRCP 26, a party is entitled to discovery of information that appears reasonably calculated to lead to the discovery of admissible evidence, as well as material that is relevant and admissible at trial.

Issue: Is a plaintiff alleging employment discrimination entitled to discover information about the firm's selection practices for other positions?

Rule: In a Title VII case in which a plaintiff alleges discriminatory employment practices, general information on the defendant's labor hierarchy is relevant within the meaning of FRCP 26.

Steffan v. Cheney (1990)

Facts: Steffan "resigned" from the U.S. Naval Academy after admitting he was a homosexual and appearing before an administrative board. He was not charged with actual homosexual conduct. Steffan filed a subsequent action challenging the constitutionality of the Naval regulations. He refused to answer deposition questions directed to whether he had engaged in homosexual conduct during his tenure.

Issue: In an action seeking judicial review of an administrative proceeding, what is the scope of discovery?

Rule: Judicial review of an administrative proceeding is confined to the grounds upon which the action was based. Hence, information that was not the basis for the administrative action is irrelevant and therefore not discoverable. Steffan challenged an administrative determination that he was unfit because he had *stated* that he was a homosexual. Therefore, whether he *engaged* in homosexual acts is irrelevant and not discoverable because it was not the basis for the administrative determination.

Hickman v. Taylor (S.Ct. 1947)

Facts: Taylor, the owner of a tugboat that sank, had obtained statements from survivors. Hickman, representing the deceased, requested copies of the statements but Taylor refused.

Issue: What written statements, private memoranda, and personal recollections may a party secure from an opponent?

Rule: (Murphy, J.) A party may secure written statements, private memoranda, and personal recollections from an opponent only if the party shows necessity or undue prejudice.

Concurrence: (Jackson, J.) Discovery should not be allowed to enable counsel to perform its functions on wits borrowed from its adversary. To rule otherwise would be to force attorneys to tell their opponent everything they have learned via their own hard work.

Bunzel Pulp & Paper Sales v. Golder (1990)

Facts: Bunzel discovered environmental contamination on land formerly owned by Golder. He filed suit to recover the clean-up expenses. Baggett discovered the contamination during routine testing. He later worked with Bunzel and its counsel in anticipation of the resulting litigation. Golder sought to depose Baggett without complying with the requirements of FRCP 26(b)(4), regarding discovery of facts known and opinions held by experts.

Issue 1: May a party's expert be deposed as a fact witness, thereby circumventing FRCP 26(b)(4)?

Rule 2: An expert may be deposed without complying with FRCP 26(b)(4) to the extent the questions are not addressed to "facts known and opinions held that were acquired or developed in anticipation of the litigation." To the extent the witness was an actor or viewer with respect to transactions or occurrences that are part of the subject matter of the lawsuit, he should be treated as an ordinary witness.

Issue 2: Can a party claim privilege in response to a general request for all relevant documents and things within the party's custody?

Rule 2: A party cannot resist discovery with a broad claim of privilege. Claims of privilege must be made on a question-by-question or document-by-document basis.

Coates v. AC & S, Inc. (1990)

Facts: After Mr. Coates expired, tissue samples were taken and sent to experts to determine the cause of death. The defendants sent the samples to experts, who were designated as experts retained in anticipation of litigation, but were not going to testify at trial. The plaintiff wished to depose the experts and obtain written reports and test results. Rule 26(b)(4) provided that a party may discover facts known or opinions held by the opposing party's experts upon a showing of exceptional circumstances under which it is impracticable to obtain the facts or opinions by other means.

Issue: When may a party compel discovery of experts consulted by the opposing party?

Rule: If each party is allowed to consult a number of experts who will disagree with each other, and only call those that will provide favorable testimony, the factfinder may be misled into thinking that professional opinion is evenly divided. The factfinder should know the extent of any disagreement among those whom a plaintiff or defendant employs. Because there is no other practicable means to obtain this information, there is an exceptional circumstance permitting discovery under FRCP 26(b)(4). Moreover, tissue samples are analogous to an autopsy, the results of which are discoverable pursuant to FRCP 35(a).

Schlagenhauf v. Holder (S.Ct. 1964)

Facts: Holder and other bus passengers involved in a collision between a Greyhound bus and a tractor-trailer sued Schlagenhauf (the bus driver), Greyhound (the bus line), Contract Carriers (the tractor owner), McCorkhill (the truck driver), and National Lead (the trailer owner). Contract Carriers and National Lead claimed the accident was due to Schlagenhauf's negligence and requested, pursuant to FRCP 35(a), that Schlagenhauf submit to four physical and mental examinations.

Issue: Under what circumstances may a court order a party to submit to mental and physical exams pursuant to FRCP 35?

Rule: (Goldberg, J.) FRCP 35 requires an affirmative showing that each condition to which an examination is sought is really and genuinely in controversy and that good cause exists for ordering each particular exam. FRCP 35 applies to all parties to the action, even if they are not party to the specific claim.

Concurrence: (Black, J.) Where allegations of a party put another party's health "in controversy," an examination may be made pursuant to FRCP 35.

Dissent: (Douglas, J.) Ordering defendants to submit to physical examination must be very limited. In an examination there is no judge present to ensure that a doctor's probing is limited only to what is relevant to the case. The right to keep one's person inviolate should not be affected simply because one has been sued.

Refac Int'l v. Hitachi, Ltd (1990)

Facts: Refac brought suit against Hitachi and numerous other defendants for patent infringement. During discovery, Refac repeatedly failed to state which of Hitachi's products were infringing and how. Consequently, judgment was entered in favor of all defendants, but the district judge declined to apply Rule 11 sanctions.

Issue: What is the standard for imposing sanctions for failure to comply with discovery requests.

Rule: To warrant imposition of severe sanctions for noncompliance with discovery requests, a court must consider 1) the public's interest in expeditious resolution of litigation; 2) the court's need to manage its docket; 3) the risk of prejudice to the defendants; 4) the public policy favoring disposition of the case on the merits; and 5) the availability of less drastic sanctions. In this case, the sanctions were proper because Refac's conduct was willful, in bad faith, and totally unjustified.

Issue 2: Do district courts have discretion to decline to apply Rule 11 sanctions?

Rule 2: A district court has discretion to choose the appropriate sanction for a Rule 11 violation. However, a court has no discretion to refuse to declare a Rule 11 violation where one has occurred.

Pressey v. Patterson (1990)

Facts: A Houston police officer frivolously shot a truck driver in the head and fabricated a story to justify the shooting. During discovery, Houston was requested to produce tapes of an interview of the Police Department's internal affairs division. After several months, Houston responded that the tape had been erased through normal reuse. At a later deposition, it was revealed that the tape was actually burned by a police spokesman. Consequently, the judge struck Houston's answer as an abuse-of-discovery sanction and granted a default judgment against it on liability.

Issue: When is it appropriate to strike a defendant's answers as a sanction for discovery misconduct?

Rule: To warrant such a severe sanction as striking a defendant's answers for improper compliance with discovery requests, the defendant must have acted in bad faith or willfully abused the judicial machinery. In this case, the court found that bad faith or willful abuse was not present because Houston did not disobey any direct court orders to produce specific evidence and because Houston posited reasonable explanations for some of the misconduct. Consequently, the severe sanctions were an abuse of discretion, although lesser sanctions were deemed appropriate.

Chapter 8

ADJUDICATION WITHOUT TRIAL

I. INTRODUCTION

Despite the constitutional right to trial by jury, a suit may very well be dismissed before opening arguments. Courts have several means for disposing of a suit before trial. Given the enormous costs of litigation, as well as the increasing delay brought about by overcrowded courts, it is not surprising that the law is more tolerant of pretrial resolution of disputes, especially if voluntary or if the suit is essentially frivolous.

II. SUMMARY JUDGMENT (FRCP 56)

A. Purposes
Summary judgment serves to:

1. Determine if a dispute exists.

2. Avoid useless trials.

3. Achieve a final determination on the merits.

4. Eliminate certain issues or claims from trial.

B. Standards and Burdens of Proof

1. Summary judgment may be granted only if there is no genuine issue of fact.

2. The moving party (the party who wants summary judgment) must be entitled to judgment as a matter of law (i.e., must have a valid legal claim).

3. The moving party has initial burden of establishing that there is no factual dispute regarding the matter upon which summary judgment is sought.

4. All doubts will be resolved against the moving party.

5. A judge will award summary judgment where a reasonable jury could not possibly decide against the moving party, according to the appropriate standard the jury would be asked to apply (preponderance of the evidence, clear and convincing evidence, or beyond a reasonable doubt).

6. No summary judgments may be entered against criminal defendants.

C. Partial Summary Judgment
A court need not dismiss the entire case. If several issues are present, but one of the issues has no genuine issue of fact, the court may summarily dismiss that claim while allowing the rest to go to trial.

III. DISMISSAL OF ACTIONS (FRCP 41)

A. Voluntary (FRCP 41(a)(1))

1. The plaintiff can voluntarily dismiss an action by filing a notice of dismissal before the defendant has served an answer.

2. The plaintiff can voluntarily dismiss an action after the defendant has answered by a stipulation signed by all parties or by leave of court.

3. The first voluntary dismissal is without prejudice to the plaintiff. This means they are not precluded from bringing the claim again later.

4. After the second voluntary dismissal, the plaintiff will be precluded from bringing another action on the same claim.

B.   Involuntary (FRCP 41(b))

1. Upon motion by the defendant, a court can order dismissal of the plaintiff's action for:

a. Failure to prosecute, or

b. Failure to comply with the FRCP.

2. An involuntary dismissal usually constitutes a judgment on the merits, except when the court dismisses without prejudice or the grounds for dismissal are:

a. Improper venue,

b. Lack of jurisdiction, or

c. Failure to join an indispensable party under FRCP 19.

IV.   DEFAULT JUDGMENTS (FRCP 55)

A.   Entry of Default

1. The clerk enters a default judgment if the defendant:

a. Does not answer the plaintiff's complaint,

b. Fails to appear at trial, or

c. Fails to comply with the FRCP.

2. If money is allegedly due, the clerk can enter a default judgment for that sum.

B.   Default Judgment

    1. A subsequent hearing may still be held to determine:

        a. Damages, or

        b. Whether the default judgment should be vacated because the defendant had a:

           i.   Valid excuse, and

           ii. A meritorious defense to the action.

    2. A motion to set aside a default judgment should be made within one year after entry.

V.   ALTERNATIVE SYSTEMS: ANALYSIS

A.   Characteristics of the Traditional System

    1. Adversarial Method
       The traditional civil proceeding involves a plaintiff and defendant whose interests are adverse. The proceedings are thus designed to use that natural animosity to encourage each side to get at the truth. However, sometimes parties do not want the truth, but a fair resolution of their dispute. Furthermore, an adversarial tack can be very damaging to a longstanding relationship that the parties may want to preserve beyond the resolution of the one dispute.

    2. Advocacy
       Professional advocates (attorneys) represent the parties in court to help them get through the often complicated legal maze. As a result, however, a client's concerns may become subordinated to the legal issues relevant to the case.

3. Adjudication

Although a judge-mandated resolution of disputes may be useful for adverse parties, in some instances it might be better to encourage parties to resolve their differences voluntarily to both parties' satisfaction. In adjudication, more often than not, one party leaves satisfied, while the other does not. In close relationships (neighbors, family, etc.) this may not be a desired result.

B. Need for Alternative Systems

1. Delay

With the massive increase in litigation in recent years, courts have been overwhelmingly backed up. Given their time constraints, many courts focus on triage-type scheduling. Criminal cases are prioritized, then cases involving the court's power of injunctive relief. As a result, many civil suits involving traditional damages may not be resolved for months, or even years.

2. Economics

Litigation gets more and more expensive every year. Although delay is responsible for much of the cost, many would-be litigants simply cannot afford the attorneys' fees.

3. Complex Litigation

Multiplicity of parties, issues, jurisdictions, and laws all present unique situations that are not readily translatable into the adversarial relationship. As such, several alternative dispute resolution methods have been generated to deal with these issues.

VI.   ALTERNATIVES

A.   Arbitration

1. Court-Ordered Arbitration
   Although most arbitration is voluntary, some states have experimented with mandated arbitration as a means of freeing much of the court docket. However, since arbitration does not grant many of the procedural protections of litigation (especially the right to a jury), it is not a widespread or favored practice of states.

2. Arbitrability

   a. By Agreement
      When looking at whether a given contractual dispute is arbitrable, courts will look first at the arbitration agreement in the contract, and construe it as broadly as possible. Almost everything relating to the contract is arbitrable, including the validity of the arbitration clause itself.

   b. Subject Matter
      Some specific matters are not generally arbitrable. These include:

      i.   Family Matters
           Including child custody, alimony, guardianship, etc.

      ii. Punitive Damages
           Some, but not all, courts have decided that punitive damages are not arbitrable on policy grounds.

      iii. Antitrust Claims
           The Supreme Court reasoned that private antitrust suits are an important part of the enforcement of antitrust policy that would be hindered through allowing arbitration of the claim. Interestingly, the

Court did not extend this reasoning to RICO claims or Securities Exchange Act violations.

iv.　Fraud in the Arbitration Agreement
Although a claim of fraud in the contract itself is arbitrable, courts will hear claims that the arbitration clause itself was fraudulently entered.

3. Procedure
Although specific arbitration associations supply their own arbitration procedure, state and federal law does not require any specific procedure.

a. Evidence
Arbitrators are free to hear or exclude any evidence they like.

b. Witnesses
They may hear from witnesses orally, in writing only, or not at all.

c. Examination
They may allow attorneys to perform all questioning, or they may participate. Cross-examinations are discretionary.

d. Opinions
They need not even write an opinion explaining their decision (and some associations discourage such opinions to prevent a court from overturning).

e. Arbitrator
One arbitrator may decide, or a panel. Dissenting and concurring opinions are neither promoted nor discouraged by law.

4. Judicial Review
Judicial review of awards are very limited, and occur only after the rendering of an arbitral award. A court will only

overturn a decision where enforcement would violate basic notions of morality and justice. However, very few situations survive this standard.

5. Enforcement
   Courts will enforce the award as long as there was some possible basis for an arbitrator to have reached that decision. There need not be an arbitral opinion.

B. Family Courts
   These courts attempt to bring about a mutually acceptable resolution of family issues, so as to lessen the adverse affects of divorce and separation on children. If mediation fails, the case may be adjudicated.

C. Small Claims
   To lessen costs to litigants, these informal courts serve to resolve disputes of less than a statutorily specified amount. The amount varies from jurisdiction to jurisdiction, depending on the state's acceptance of this form of dispute resolution (which often varies proportionally to the backlog in civil courts).

D. Negotiations
   Many court have rules designed to encourage settlement of disputes before trial. However, a judge must be careful not to favor one side too heavily, thus impinging on rules regarding impartiality.

E. Local Resolution
   Some jurisdictions have set up neighborhood courts that informally mediate disputes between neighbors, spouses, and local merchants in close neighborhoods. This serves to maintain a sense of community and stability, as well as offer individualized remedies. Mediators are given wide discretion in arriving at a mutually acceptable solution. If a solution cannot be found, the dispute may then be litigated in court.

F.   Rent-A-Judge
A favorite of complex litigation, all parties split the cost of hiring a retired judge to act as a more formal arbitrator of their dispute. Often, but not always, the proceedings are held with many of the rules of civil procedure and evidence, hybridized from the various jurisdictions.

G.   Other Countries
Foreign nations have different philosophies of jurisprudence. Civil law countries, for instance, are governed almost entirely by statute, with little or no common law. Many countries do not have trials, judges take an active role in questioning parties, and witnesses may appear seldom or only in writing. Some commentators have advocated that certain of these rules or approaches be transplanted into the American system.

VII.   PRETRIAL CONFERENCE

A.   Purposes
A pretrial conference is used for trial preparation to:

1. Clarify issues.

2. Amend pleadings.

3. Identify witnesses and documents.

4. Discuss settlement or extrajudicial procedures (i.e., alternate dispute resolutions, special proceedings).

B.   Scheduling
In most cases, a judge is required to issue a scheduling order within 120 days after the complaint is filed.

C.   Limits
A pretrial conference may not be used to:

1. Serve as a substitute for trial.

2. Steal opponent's trial preparation.

VIII. PRETRIAL ORDER

A. Purposes
A pretrial order serves to:

1. Document the issues agreed upon at the pretrial conference.

2. Control the parties' courses of action.

B. Effects
Failure to comply with the pretrial order can result in:

1. Striking of pleadings or defenses.

2. Exclusion of evidence at trial.

3. Dismissal of action.

4. Mistrial.

5. Attorney's fees.

CASE CLIPS

Peralta v. Heights Medical Center (S.Ct. 1988)
Facts: Heights Medical center sued Peralta, alleging that he had guaranteed the debt of one of his employees. Peralta did not appear or answer, claiming that he was not properly served with process. A default judgment was entered against him and a lien was placed on his real property, which fetched a deflated price at auction. Peralta appealed, claiming that his due process rights were violated. The Texas courts rejected Peralta's appeals because

he did not show that he had a meritorious defense (i.e., retrial might produce a different judgment).

Issue: May a state require that an appellant who seeks review for a due process violation must show that he had a meritorious defense to the original claim?

Rule: (White, J.) To require an appellant who has been deprived of property in a manner contrary to due process to show that he had a meritorious defense to the original action violates the Due Process Clause of the Fourteenth Amendment.

Manshack v. Southwestern Electric Power Co. (1990)

Facts: Manshack sued Southwestern Electric ["SWEPCO"] in Texas federal court for injuries he sustained while working on a high voltage wire. The court ruled that Louisiana law would apply, thereby limiting Manshack's recovery to workman's compensation. Manshack successfully moved for voluntary dismissal so that he could refile in state court where more favorable law might (or might not) apply. SWEPCO appealed, maintaining that the ruling caused them to suffer clear legal prejudice.

Issue: Does granting voluntary dismissal so that a case can be transferred prejudice a defendant?

Rule: Granting voluntary dismissal so that a case can be transferred may prejudice a defendant if it strips the defendant of an absolute defense, but not where, as here, it merely subjects the defendant to a second suit under the same choice-of-law rules.

Celotex Corp. v. Catrett (S.Ct. 1986)

Facts: Catrett alleged that her husband died as a result of exposure to asbestos manufactured by Celotex. Catrett sued for negligence, breach of warranty, and strict liability. Celotex moved for summary judgment under FRCP 56 on the grounds that Catrett has not offered any evidence to support the allegation that her husband had been exposed to Celotex products. Catrett argued that Celotex had to produce evidence negating the allegation that her husband had been exposed.

Issue: Must a party submit evidence to support a FRCP 56 motion for summary judgment?

Rule: (Rehnquist, J.) If the opposing party's briefs themselves satisfy the standard for summary judgment, the motion will be granted even if the motion was not supported by affidavits.

Concurrence: (White, J.) It is the defendant's task to negate the claimed basis for the suit.

Dissent: (Brennan, J.) The court sets out no identifiable standard for the granting of summary judgment. Where, as here, the party making the motion for summary judgment would also have to carry the burden of persuasion at trial, that party must support its motion with credible evidence.

Visser v. Packer Eng'g Assoc.

Facts: Visser had sided with other employees in a recent battle. Packer called Visser into his office and demanded his loyalty. Visser refused and demanded an apology from Packer. Packer immediately fired him. Because this occurred nine months before Visser would have been eligible for full pension benefits, Visser brought an age discrimination suit. The court granted Packer's motion for summary judgement on the ground that there was no evidence that age or pension cost played a factor in the firing of Visser.

Issue: When should summary judgment be granted on the basis of inadequate evidence to support a claim?

Rule: Summary judgment is appropriate if, based on the evidence presented in the summary judgment proceeding, no rational jury could reach a verdict for the party opposing summary judgment.

Dissent: Summary judgment is inappropriate in this case because there are material issues of fact from which a jury could find that there was age discrimination.

Ferguson v. Writers Guild of America, West (1991)

Facts: Ferguson was hired to write the screenplay for Beverly Hills Cop II. Members of the Writers Guild agreed that the task of determining the relative contributions of the various writers would be handled by Writers Guild committees. When the picture was completed, the Writers Guild determined that Ferguson should share credit for the screenplay; credit for the story was given to two others. The Writers Guild had elaborate rules for making such determinations and arbitrating subsequent disputes. After Ferguson was unsuccessful in the arbitration proceedings, he brought suit in state court.

Issue: What is the scope of judicial review of arbitration proceedings?

Rule: Where parties have agreed among themselves to bring a matter before a specially skilled arbitration committee and not to litigate the matter, judicial review is limited to whether the arbitrators exceeded their powers and whether the procedures employed deprived the objecting party of a fair opportunity to be heard.

Lockhart v. Patel (1987)

Facts: A teenager who lost an eye brought a medical malpractice action. After several formal and informal pretrial conferences, the judge ordered the defense counsel to bring a representative, "not some flunky," from the insurance company who was authorized to enter into a settlement. They sent a flunky. Consequently, the court struck the defendant's pleadings and declared him in default.

Issue: May a court order parties and their insurers to attend settlement conferences?

Rule: FRCP 16 authorizes courts to order parties and their liability insurers to attend settlement conferences, and to impose sanctions for disregarding such orders.

McKey v. Fairbairn (1965)

Facts: Water leaked into the house McKey rented from Fairbairn, allegedly causing McKey's mother-in-law to slip and fall. The pretrial order set forth an allegation of negligence for failure to repair and eliminate a dangerous condition after receiving notice. During the trial, McKey sought to amend the pretrial order to permit him to introduce local housing regulations that required roofs and walls to be leakproof. Although the landlord was aware of these regulations, the trial court did not permit the plaintiff to change recovery theories.

Issue: May a plaintiff depart from a pretrial order and present a new theory of recovery at trial?

Rule: Where a plaintiff has not presented a particular theory of recovery until trial, refusing to permit the appellant to change her theory is within the judge's discretion.

Dissent: Whether a plaintiff should be permitted to establish a new theory of recovery during trial is determined by balancing the possible prejudice to the defendant against the injustice that would be prevented by permitting the modification. Because the defendants in this case knew of the regulations, their disadvantage would be small in comparison with the injustice the plaintiff would suffer if relevant evidence is precluded.

Chapter 9

TRIAL

I. BURDEN OF PROOF

A. Burden of Production
    Each party must produce sufficient evidence to prevent a
    directed verdict.

    1. The plaintiff bears the initial burden, then the defendant
       must rebut the plaintiff's evidence.

    2. The defendant submitting affirmative defenses bears the
       burden of proving that defense, but the plaintiff may then
       rebut.

B. Burden of Persuasion

    1. The plaintiff (or the defendant asserting an affirmative de-
       fense) must persuade the jury (or judge) of the existence
       of the facts claimed.

    2. Generally, the burden is met where a party establishes by
       a preponderance of evidence (i.e., more likely than not)
       that the events occurred as claimed.

    3. However, stronger burdens may be applied in certain
       cases.

       a. Clear and Convincing
          This stricter standard is most often used where person-
          al reputation is at stake, such as libel and slander cases.
          This standard also applies to many aspects of family
          law as well as probate litigation.

b. Beyond a Reasonable Doubt
This standard is rarely used in civil cases, since it is the highest burden available at law. It is typically used in criminal cases.

C. Presumptions

1. A presumption is a rule of law holding that when a basic fact is found, another fact is presumed to exist, absent rebuttal.

2. Various types of presumptions exist. Some may be used to satisfy burdens of production; others may not. Some may be used to satisfy burdens of persuasion; others may not. Some presumptions may be mere inferences, not enough on their own to satisfy a burden, but capable of being considered with other evidence.

II. JURY TRIAL

A. Demand For Jury Trial (FRCP 38)
Must be served on all parties not later than ten days after service of last pleading.

B. Jury Selection

1. Voir Dire

a. Each party's counsel questions potential jurors to discover possible bias.

b. Judge may also pose questions.

2. Juror Dismissal

a. Provided dismissal does not violate Fourteenth Amendment (i.e., solely motivated by racial consideration, etc.), each side's lawyer has unlimited challenges for cause (i.e., bias) to juror's suitability to hear case.

b. Each litigant gets three peremptory challenges (i.e., cause need not be shown).

C.   Jury's Role
Juries decide factual issues only.

1. Basic facts
The occurrence or nonoccurrence of a fact which does not itself prove one of the necessary elements of the claim or defense.

2. Ultimate fact
Established basic facts that prove a party's claim.

D.   Jury Charge

1. Judge instructs jury as to the doctrine relevant to a party's claim and its application to factual findings.

2. Each party may submit to the judge instructions the party wants read to jury.

3. Judge's failure to submit correct instruction is reversible error if it prejudices verdict.

E.   Unanimity (FRCP 48)
The verdict must be unanimous unless parties stipulate that a stated majority shall deliver the verdict.

F.   Right to Jury Trial

1. Seventh Amendment

a. Guarantees jury trial in actions triable at law.

b. Nonjury cases

i.   Actions in equity and cases where a jury is waived are tried before a judge.

    ii. Trial judge must make specific factual findings and legal conclusions, clearly and distinctly stating both.

2. Mixed Legal and Equitable Claims

    a. In federal court, where legal issues are incidental to equitable issues, a right to jury trial for legal issues exists (most state courts hold jury trial waived in this situation).

    b. In federal court, where legal issues are not incidental to the equitable issue, the legal issue is tried before a jury (preferably prior to the equitable issue), and the equitable issue is tried before a judge.

3. Statutory Actions and Administrative Proceedings

    a. Congress has broad power to create a statutory right to jury trial where none existed in common law.

    b. A right to jury trial does not extend to administrative proceedings.

4. State Law Right to Jury Trial

    a. Diversity cases
       If state law disallows jury trials where federal law would permit them, federal law controls.

    b. Federal issues in state courts
       A party pressing a federal issue in state court is entitled to a jury if federal law mandates a jury trial.

III.   DISPOSITION

A.   Nonsuit
If after the plaintiff presents his case, he fails to show a right to relief, her case is dismissed. (The test is same as for directed verdicts.)

B. Judgment as a Matter of Law (FRCP 50)
Effective as of December 1, 1991, judgment as a matter of law encompasses the motions previously known as directed verdict and judgment notwithstanding the verdict (JNOV).

1. Directed Verdict

a. Takes case away from jury.

b. The defendant may move for a directed verdict at the close of the plaintiff's case-in-chief; either party may move for a directed verdict when all the evidence is in.

c. Judge views the evidence in the most favorable light to whoever opposes the directed verdict.

d. The motion will be granted where:

i. There exists insufficient evidence to go to jury; or

ii. The evidence is such that reasonable people could not differ as to the result.

2. Judgment Notwithstanding the Verdict (JNOV)

a. The judge substitutes his verdict for that of jury's.

b. A party must move for a directed verdict before a motion for a JNOV is submitted.

c. The same standard is applied as with the directed verdict.

C. Motion for a New Trial
Courts have broad discretion in ordering new trials; they may be granted based on either questions of law or fact.

1. Grounds

    a. Misconduct of judge or lawyers.

    b. Juror discovered evidence.

    c. Newly discovered evidence.

    d. Insufficient evidence to support judgment or verdict.

    e. Error in law (e.g., evidentiary rulings, erroneous jury charge).

2. Partial New Trial
Where liability is clearly established, courts can order new trials regarding a damage award that is considered inappropriate.

D. Motion for Relief From Judgment (FRCP 60)

1. Defined
A motion granted where a party is prevented from presenting a full case.

2. Grounds for Reopening a Case

    a. Mistake or excusable neglect.

    b. Newly discovered evidence.

    c. Judgment satisfied or underlying prior judgment is void, reversed, or vacated.

    d. Fraud or misrepresentation of a litigant.

    e. Any other reason advancing the interests of justice.

3. Other Considerations

    a. The motion will be granted only where a substantial right is prejudiced.

    b. The court may correct errors made by a clerk entering judgment.

IV. VERDICTS

A. General Verdict

1. The jury finds for a party and grants relief without articulating specific factual findings.

2. The implication is that all essential issues were found in favor of the prevailing party.

3. There exists the potential to conceal jury's misunderstandings of fact, etc.

B. General Verdict With Interrogatories

1. Jury is instructed to deliver a general verdict as well as answers to questions regarding essential factual findings and issues.

2. Purpose

    a. Ensures that the jury considered essential facts and issues.

    b. Permits the court to verify the accuracy of verdict by comparing the verdict with the jury's answers to see if they are consistent.

3. Generally, if the answers to the interrogatory are consistent with each other but inconsistent with the general

verdict, the answers control (court may also grant new trial or direct the jury to deliberate further).

4. If the answers are inconsistent among themselves and some are inconsistent with the verdict, a new trial results.

5. The court must try to harmonize the general verdict with the jury's answers.

C. Special Verdicts (FRCP 49(a))

1. Juries make factual findings only.

2. Judges apply the law to the juries' factual findings and render a verdict.

D. Erroneous Verdicts

1. Failure by a jury to follow instructions may be grounds to set the verdict aside (e.g., a compromise verdict is erroneous).

2. An internally inconsistent verdict results when jury findings are inconsistent and irreconcilable (e.g., jury holds employer liable under respondent superior, yet finds employee acted with due care).

3. If an erroneous verdict is correctable, a court abuses its discretion if, upon motion, it fails to direct further jury deliberations.

4. Errors are waived unless the prejudiced party timely objects; errors that do not prejudice a substantial right are held harmless.

E. Contempt Orders

1. The property of the judgment debtor is seized.

2. Only that amount of property sufficient to cover the judgment may be levied.

3. Civil contempt of court

    a. A party returns to court to show the other party's noncompliance with the judgment.

    b. A noncomplying party held in contempt may be fined, imprisoned, or both until compliance results.

CASE CLIPS

Chauffeurs, Teamsters & Helpers, Local No. 391 v. Terry (S.Ct. 1990)

Facts: Workers filed grievances with their union regarding layoffs at a trucking company. When the union would not prosecute the grievances, the workers sought back pay from the union for breaching its duty of fair representation. Because the cause of action had legal (breach of contract) and equitable (breach of fiduciary duty) elements, a dispute arose as to whether the plaintiffs were entitled to a jury trial. There is generally no right to a jury for claims based in equity.

Issue: In a claim that raises legal and equitable issues, is a plaintiff entitled to a jury trial?

Rule: (Marshall, J.) When it is not clear whether a claim is legal or equitable, whether a plaintiff is entitled to a jury trial depends on whether the remedy sought is legal or equitable in nature. If the remedy sought is of the type traditionally awarded by courts of law, a plaintiff is entitled to a jury title under the Seventh Amendment. Thus, a request for money damages will typically entitle plaintiffs to a jury trial, as was the case here. However, money damages may be characterized as equitable in situations where they are restitutionary or incidental to injunctive relief.

Dissent: (Kennedy, J.) The majority is correct in its formulation of the guiding rule of law. However, a fair representation suit most resembles an equitable trust actions.

Atlas Roofing Co. v. Occupational Safety and Health Review Commission (S.Ct. 1977)

Facts: In 1970, Congress passed the Occupational Safety and Heath Act (OSHA) authorizing the Labor Department to require employers to correct unsafe working conditions, and imposing civil penalties on employers who did not comply. Any disputes were handled before an administrative law judge, and never before a jury.

Issue: May Congress create a cause of action for civil penalties that may be litigated only in an administrative agency that does not provide for a jury trial?

Rule: (White, J.) The Seventh Amendment applies to all suits "at common law." This does not prevent Congress from assigning suits of the sort normally tried by a jury before an agency instead, if the suit involves new statutes creating "public rights."

Granfinanciera, S.A. v. Nordberg (S.Ct. 1989)

Facts: Nordberg sued Granfinanciera to recover funds transferred to it by a bankruptcy debtor. Granfinanciera was denied a jury trial on the grounds that bankruptcy courts are non-Article III tribunals, which are not governed by the Seventh Amendment.

Issue: Is there a right to a jury in cases being adjudicated by non-Article III courts?

Rule: If Congress creates new causes of action involving public rights, it may assign their adjudication to tribunals that do not use juries as factfinders. However, Congress may not block application of the Seventh Amendment to private-right cases (e.g., tort, contract, property, and other suits at common law). A bankruptcy trustee's right to recover a fraudulent conveyance most nearly resembles a state-law contract claim, which carries with it a right to a jury trial.

Beacon Theatres v. Westover (S.Ct. 1959)

Facts: Fox West Coast Theatres, Inc. sued Beacon Theatres, Inc., asking for a declaratory statement that it was not violating antitrust laws, and an injunction stopping Beacon from threatening Fox with antitrust suits. The declaratory and injunctive claims are both in equity, and do not receive juries. Beacon counterclaimed, alleging violation of antitrust laws and requested a jury trial pursuant to FRCP 38(b).

Issue: Is a right to a jury trial lost because the only issues for which a jury may be requested occur as part of a counterclaim?

Rule: (Black, J.) Under the FRCP, the right to a jury trial is not precluded merely because the case presents both legal and equitable issues. The same court may try both legal and equitable issues in the same action.

Dissent: (Stewart, J.) FRCP 42(b) allows the judge to hear legal and equitable issues in any manner the judge sees fit. The presence of a legal issue should not destroy another party's equitable suit.

McDonough Power Equipment, Inc. v. Greenwood (S.Ct. 1984)

Facts: Greenwood sued when he was injured while using McDonough Power Equipment's equipment. After a jury verdict for McDonough, Greenwood learned that the jury foreman failed to answer a question during voir dire that may have revealed prejudice.

Issue: Is a party entitled to a new trial because a juror failed to answer a question during voir dire?

Rule: (Rehnquist, J.) The party seeking a new trial must show that the juror failed to honestly answer a material question during voir dire and that a correct response would have provided a valid basis to a challenge for cause (the motives for concealing information may vary, but only those reasons that affect a juror's impartiality can truly be said to affect the fairness of a trial).

Concurrence 1: (Blackmun, J.) Regardless of whether a juror's answer is honest or dishonest, it remains within a trial court's option, in determining whether a jury was biased, to order a posttrial hearing at which the challenging party has the opportunity to demonstrate actual bias or, in exceptional circumstances, that the facts are such that bias is to be inferred.

Concurrence 2: (Brennan, J.) To be awarded a new trial, a litigant should be required to demonstrate that the juror incorrectly responded to a material question on voir dire, and that, under the facts and circumstances surrounding the particular case, the juror was biased against the moving litigant.

Edmonson v. Leesville Concrete Co. (S.Ct. 1991)

Facts: The defendant in a negligence action brought by an African-American used peremptory challenges to strike prospective African-American jurors. The plaintiff claimed that the defendant must provide a race-neutral explanation for the peremptory strikes.
Issue: May a private litigant in a civil case use peremptory challenges to exclude jurors on account of their race?
Rule: (Kennedy, J.) Peremptory challenges exist only because the government permits them. Peremptory challenges are thus attributable to the government, even when exercised by a private attorney. Therefore, use of peremptory challenges to exclude jurors on account of their race violates the jurors' equal protection rights.
Dissent: (O'Connor, J.) The state does not significantly participate in the peremptory challenge process, and the exercise of a peremptory challenge is not a traditional government function. Because racially motivated peremptory challenges are not state actions, they do not violate the Fifth Amendment.

Liljeberg v. Health Services Acquisition Corp. (S.Ct. 1988)

Facts: After a trial without a jury, the judge ruled for Liljeberg, the defendant. The Health Services Acquisition Corporation then learned that the judge had been on a board of trustees with which Liljeberg had been negotiating to purchase a large piece of land. The success of the negotiations turned, in large part, on Liljeberg prevailing against Health Services Acquisition. The judge did not know of any conflict of interest at the time of trial or judgment.
Issue: When may a judge be disqualified under FRCP 60(b)(6)?
Rule: (Stewart, J.) Where the judge knows that he, individually or as a fiduciary, has a financial interest in the subject matter or in a party to a proceeding, he should recuse himself. Here the judge clearly should have done so.
Dissent: (Rehnquist, C.J.) An otherwise valid judgment should not be overturned because of a conflict of interest that could not have affected the judge's decisionmaking ability.

Reid v. San Pedro, Los Angeles & Salt Lake Railroad (1911)
Facts: Reid's cow was killed when it strayed into the path of an oncoming train. The cow could have wandered onto the track through either a hole in the railroad's fence or an open gate to Reid's pasture.
Issue: What standard of proof is required in a negligence case?
Rule: A plaintiff must prove negligence by a preponderance of the evidence.

Pennsylvania Railroad v. Chamberlain (S.Ct. 1933)
Facts: At trial, the judge directed a verdict for Chamberlain even though the proven facts gave equal support to both the railroad's and Chamberlain's allegations.
Issue: May a judge direct a verdict where the evidence could support either party's allegations?
Rule: (Sutherland, J.)   Where evidence could support either party's allegations, judgment must go against the party that had the burden of proof.

Railroad Co. v. Stout (S.Ct. 1873)
Facts: At trial, the judge charged the jury with instructions on determining whether the railroad was negligent. The jury then found for Stout.
Issue: May a judge charge a jury with determining whether a party was negligent?
Rule: (Hunt, J.)   The question of negligence is one properly charged to the jury, and if it is reasonable that the jury could find negligence, the decision must stand.

Trezza v. Dame (1967)
Facts: In an action to recover personal injuries resulting from a car crash, the judge commented to the jury, "[I]t is rather clear in this case that the defendant is negligent and her negligence was responsible for the accident. . . ." and, "I do not think there is any issue of fact. . . ." He did, however, inform the jury that they could disagree with his opinion.
Issue: May a trial judge make comments that suggest to the jury how they should resolve factual issues?

Rule: A judge may comment on evidence and express his opinion on factual issues, but a judge may not pronounce his opinion on ultimate issues so forcefully that he usurps the function of the jury. In the instant case, the appellate court did not approve of the judge's comments, but did not find that they were sufficiently prejudicial to warrant reversal because his opinions seemed correct.

In re Beverly Hills Fire Litigation (1982)

Facts: In a suit resulting from a fire, it was alleged that a certain type of wiring had caused the fire. Concerned by an expert's characterization of the wire as "a time bomb," a juror inspected and experimented with the wiring in his house. The experiment yielded results that contradicted evidence in the case. The plaintiff moved for a mistrial.

Issue: May jurors conduct private experiments?

Rule: Jurors may not conduct experiments outside the courtroom because such experiments constitute additional evidence that is not subject to scrutiny or cross-examination. Such evidence is prejudicial and is grounds for reversal if it had any influence on the jury's deliberations or verdict. The juror's motivation for conducting the experiment is not relevant.

Lind v. Schenley Indus. (1960)

Facts: After hearing conflicting testimony as to the existence of a contract, a jury found that an oral contract existed. The trial judge did not agree and granted a new trial.

Issue: What is the standard for setting aside a jury's verdict as contrary to the weight of the evidence?

Rule: A trial judge has wide discretion to grant a new trial if a possibly erroneous verdict resulted from circumstances beyond the jury's control (e.g., improperly admitted evidence, prejudicial statements by counsel, or an improper charge). It is an abuse of discretion for a judge to set aside a jury verdict simply because he has reached a different conclusion. The degree of judicial scrutiny should vary with the subject of the litigation. Closer scrutiny of a verdict is warranted when the case deals with complex and specialized subject matter, but the jury's judgment should control on issues such as the veracity of witnesses.

Neely v. Martin K. Eby Construction Co.
(S.Ct. 1967)

Facts: Neely won a jury verdict in district court over both directed verdict and motions for a judgment notwithstanding the verdict (JNOV) by Martin K. Eby Construction Co. On appeal, the court reversed the denial of Marin's JNOV motion and dismissed the action.

Issue: Must an appellate court grant a new trial rather than dismiss an action if it determines that the prevailing party's evidence was insufficient to sustain a verdict?

Rule: (White, J.) FRCP 50(d) states that the prevailing party has the right to urge an appellate court to order a new trial rather than set aside a verdict. This rule does not mean, however, that the appellate court must order a new trial in such a case. Hence, appellate courts can enter a JNOV, provided the party prevailing at trial first has an opportunity to establish grounds for a new trial.

Dissent 1: (Douglas, J.) Although the court's interpretation of FRCP 50 was correct, in this case the jury's verdict should nevertheless stand.

Dissent 2: (Black, J.) Whenever a jury verdict is overturned, for whatever reason, the losing party must have an opportunity to request a new jury trial.

Tittle v. Aldacosta (1977)

Facts: Aldacosta fell when disembarking from Tittle's boat. It was the usual practice to put down a towel to prevent disembarking passengers from slipping. The towel was not in place when Aldacosta was injured. In a bench trial, the judge found that the absent towel was not the proximate cause of Aldacosta's injuries and that the accident was not caused by negligence on the part of the owner, the crew, or the vessel. The appellate court disagreed.

Issue: What is the standard for setting aside a judge's findings of fact?

Rule: A judge's findings of fact will only be set aside if clearly erroneous. However, because a judge's factfinding role does not implicate the same Seventh Amendment concerns as jury trials, the reviewing court can be less deferential to judicial findings than jury findings.

Chapter 10

APPEAL

I. FINAL JUDGMENT RULE

A. Generally

    1. For the most part, only final judgments are appealable.

    2. A final judgment is reached when, on the merits, litigation ends, leaving only the execution of judgment to be completed.

    3. Substance, not form, determines if a judgment is final.

B. Interlocutory Appeals Exception
Interlocutory appeals are allowed in cases involving:

    1. Collateral Orders
A collateral order is one which:

        a. Raises serious legal questions;

        b. Involves a danger of irreparable harm; and

        c. Deals with an issue unrelated to the basic substantive claims asserted.

    2. Multiple Claims or Parties
A final decision as to one or more, but less than all, the claims or parties before the court may be appealed before all claims of all parties have been resolved.

    3. Equitable Orders
E.g., grant, denial, or modification of an injunction.

4. Questions of Great Import
   If a trial judge certifies, and the appellate court agrees, that the order involves a controlling question of law over which a difference of opinion exists, and that immediate appeal may materially advance termination of the litigation, an interlocutory appeal will be allowed.

5. Possibility of Irreparable Harm
   Courts admit interlocutory appeals of orders affecting substantial rights that will be lost if not immediately appealed.

6. Writs of Mandamus or Prohibition

   a. When Used
      Appellate courts may grant a writ only if the trial court exceeds its jurisdiction or clearly abuses its discretion.

   b. Factors
      When deciding a petition for a writ a court will consider:

      Mnemonic: **PLACE**

      i.   Prejudice
           Whether petitioner will be prejudiced in a manner not correctable on appeal;

      ii. Law of First Impression
           Whether the district court's order raises important issues of law of first impression;

      iii. Adequate Alternate Relief
           Whether petitioner has other adequate means to obtain relief;

      iv. Clearly Erroneous Errors
           Whether the district court's order is, as a matter of law, clearly erroneous; or

      v. Error That Is Often Repeated
         Whether the district court's order is an oft-repeated error or a manifest persistent disregard of the FRCP;

II.   PROCEDURES

A.   Timeliness
The time period in which an appeal must be brought begins to run once judgment is entered.

B.   Standing to Appeal

    1. Only a party injured (or aggrieved) by the judgment of the lower court has standing to appeal.

    2. It is possible for both parties to be injured by a single judgment. Simply because one party is injured less does not mean they cannot appeal.

    3. Nonparties may not appeal.

C.   Notice of Appeal

    1. Notice of appeal must be filed within thirty days (sixty days if the United States is a party) of the judgment's entry.

    2. If a court finds excusable neglect or good cause, a thirty-day extension to file a notice of appeal will be granted.

    3. Parties to a suit cannot stipulate to alter the time within which to take an appeal.

D.   Waiver
A party may expressly or impliedly waive any right to appeal.

E. Rehearing
A court (the Supreme Court, or Circuit Courts en banc), at its discretion, may order a rehearing of a case if:

1. The petition is timely filed; or

2. The strict application of the rules favoring finality of judgments would unfairly impinge on the interests of justice.

III. SCOPE OF REVIEW

A. Reviewable Issues
Generally, appellate courts only review issues of law, not factual findings.

B. Jury Trials

1. An appellate court must uphold a verdict supported by substantial evidence.

2. An appellate court cannot weigh evidence or pass on witness credibility.

3. An appellate court cannot disturb factual findings.

C. Nonjury Trials

1. If clearly erroneous, a judge's factual findings may be set aside.

2. Questions of witness credibility are solely in the trial court's province.

D. Errors
Appellate courts have jurisdiction only if an error:

1. Involves a legal issue;

2. Appears in the trial record;

3. Affects a substantial right of the aggrieved party; and

4. Is preserved by prompt objection to a court's ruling.

E.   Harmless Error
When an error neither prejudices a substantial right of the aggrieved party nor has a significant effect on a case's outcome, courts will not reverse a judgment.

IV.   HIGH COURTS

A.   Generally
Every state has its high court, generally known as the State Supreme Court, although each state will have its own title. The federal court is of course led by the United States Supreme Court. Intermediate appellate courts generally exist to relieve the burdens of the high courts, but there are exceptions to every rule.

B.   Original Jurisdiction
Every jurisdiction delineates certain areas of the law where the high court has original jurisdiction. In other words, an appeal under original jurisdiction must, as of right, go straight to the top.

C.   Discretionary Review

1. Generally
According to Chief Justice Taft, there is no right to appeal all the way to the top. The Supreme Court's function is not primarily to preserve the rights of the litigants. It is to expound and stabilize principles of law. Most state systems express the same view.

2. Certiorari
The Supreme Court exercises its discretionary power by granting writs of certiorari. By requiring certification of a case before hearing it, the Court can select those cases it feels most compelled to decide.

a. Rule of Four
   It takes a vote of only four of the nine justices to grant
   writ. In contrast, it normally requires five justices to
   decide a case.

b. Factors
   In determining whether to grant a petition for certiorari, the justices will consider:

   i. State Court Deciding Federal Law
       Where a state court is the first to interpret a federal
       law, or misinterprets it.

   ii. Conflict in Court of Appeals
       The Circuits are in conflict with each other or with
       the decisions of state courts.

CASE CLIPS

Aetna Casualty & Surety Co. v. Yeatts (1941)

Facts: Aetna Casualty sued for a declaratory judgment that its insured, Yeatts, was not covered for liability resulting from criminal-
ly-performed abortions. Following a jury verdict for Yeatts, Aetna
Casualty unsuccessfully moved for a judgment notwithstanding
the verdict and then moved for a new trial.

Issue: Can a judge order a new trial even if the weight of the evidence would not have supported a directed verdict?

Rule: A judge can grant a new trial if he is of the opinion that the
verdict is against the clear weight of the evidence, is based upon
evidence which is false, or will result in a miscarriage of justice.

Carson Products Co. v. Califano (1979)

Facts: Carson filed suit in district court too challenge an FDA
determination that an ingredient in Carson's shaving powder was
not entitled to trade secret protection. After judgment was
rendered, it was determined in *Zotos International v. Kennedy* that

FDA procedures violated due process. The FDA modified its procedures in response to the decision. Carson then brought this appeal which raised a new due process attack on FDA procedures.
Issue: May a party raise an argument for the first time on appeal?
Rule: Although parties are generally not permitted to raise issues on appeal that were not raised at trial, a court of appeals has authority to hear an issue not raised at trial in exceptional circumstances where injustice might otherwise result. A dramatic change in the legal climate that occurred subsequent to a district court decision is such an exceptional circumstance.

Massachusetts Mut. Life Ins. Co. v. Ludwig (S.Ct. 1976)

Facts: In a case for payment on an insurance policy, the district court held that under Illinois conflict-of-law rules, Michigan law applied. In an appeal brought by Ludwig, Massachusetts Mutual argued that Illinois conflict-of-law rules actually required application of Illinois law. The appeals court held that Massachusetts Mutual could not argue that Illinois law applied because it had not cross-appealed from the district court's ruling that Michigan law applied.
Issue: May an appellee who has not cross-appealed attack a ruling of the lower court?
Rule: (Per Curiam) A party who does not appeal from a final decree of a trial court may not attack the decree to correct an error or to supplement the decree with a matter not dealt with below. However, when the party only seeks to attack the reasoning of the lower court, a cross-appeal is not a necessary prerequisite. Massachusetts Mutual's argument that Illinois law applied was no more than an attack on the reasoning of the court.

Liberty Mutual Insurance Co. v. Wetzel
(S.Ct. 1976)

Facts: Wetzel and others alleged that Liberty Mutual's employee insurance benefits and maternity leave regulations discriminated against women in violation of Title VII of the Civil Rights Act of 1964. The district court granted partial summary judgment for Wetzel solely on the issue of liability, without considering the issue of relief. Liberty Mutual appealed under 28 U.S.C. § 1291.

Issue 1: May an order for partial summary judgment limited to the issue of liability alone be appealed under 28 U.S.C. § 1291?

Rule 1: (Rehnquist, J.) A partial summary judgment order solely on the issue of liability is not a "final decision" as required by 28 U.S.C. § 1291.

Issue 2: May an order for partial summary judgment limited to the issue of liability be appealed under 28 U.S.C. § 1292(a)(1)?

Rule 2: Interlocutory appeals under 28 U.S.C. § 1292(a)(1) are limited to review of injunctive relief. Where, as here, no injunctive relief has been granted, a party may not appeal a district court's order under this section.

Lauro Lines s.r.l. v. Chasser (S.Ct. 1989)

Facts: The plaintiffs brought suit in district court to recover damages they sustained while passengers aboard the Achille Lauro, which was hijacked by terrorists. Lauro Lines moved to dismiss, citing a forum selection clause printed on each passenger ticket that required all suits be brought in Italy. The district court declined to enforce the clause. The court of appeals would not hear Lauro Lines' appeal on the ground that the district court's order denying the motion was interlocutory (not a final judgment that ends the litigation on the merits). There is a narrow exception to the final judgment rule, the collateral order doctrine, which allows a party to appeal an interlocutory order if the asserted right would be destroyed if not vindicated before trial.

Issue: Does an order denying a motion to dismiss for improper forum fall under the collateral order exception to the final judgment rule?

Rule: (Brennan, J.) An order denying a motion to dismiss on the basis of a forum-selection clause does not fall under the collateral order exception to the final judgment rule. The potential costs associated with failure to enforce a forum selection clause (e.g., the expense of relitigating the matter in the proper forum) are not sufficient to warrant immediate appeal.

Concurrence: (Scalia, J.) The result in this case is correct because contractual forum selection is not a sufficiently *important* right to warrant immediate review.

Garner v. Wolfinbarger (1970)

Facts: Plaintiffs sued a corporation in which they were shareholders for a variety of violations in the Northern District of Alabama. The court transferred the case to the Southern District of Alabama under § 1404 (change of venue). The plaintiffs sought review of the transfer order by interlocutory appeal under § 1292(b). Section 1292(b) permits interlocutory appeals for the purpose of resolving a controlling issue of law as to which there is substantial ground for a difference of opinion.

Issue: Is a transfer order subject to interlocutory review under § 1292(b)?

Rule: Section 1292(b) review is inappropriate for challenges to a judge's discretion in granting or denying changes of venue under § 1404. It might be appropriate if the movants were claiming that the district judge failed to correctly construe the statute, but such is not the case here.

Kerr v. U.S. District Court (S.Ct. 1976)

Facts: Several California inmates brought a class action against several state agencies. The agencies sought an issuance of writs of mandamus to compel the district court to vacate two discovery orders. The court of appeals refused to issue the mandamus.

Issue: When should a court issue a writ of mandamus?

Rule: (Marshall, J.) Writs of mandamus should be granted only where no other adequate remedies are available.

Anderson v. Bessemer City (S.Ct. 1985)

Facts: The district court found that Bessemer City had denied Ms. Anderson employment in favor of Mr. Kincaid because of her sex. The court's decision was based on the following subsidiary findings: Anderson was better qualified than Kincaid; male hiring committee members were biased against Anderson because she was a woman; only Anderson was asked if her spouse would object to her taking the job; and the reasons offered by the committee for choosing Kincaid were pretextual. The appellate court conducted a de novo weighing of the evidence in the record and concluded that Kincaid was indeed better qualified for the job.

Issue: When may an appellate court reverse a trial court's findings of fact?

Rule: (White, J.) An appellate court may only reverse a trial court's findings of fact when they are clearly erroneous. Where the trial court and the appellate court reach different, but equally logical, conclusions from the evidence, the interpretation of the trial court controls. Because the findings of the trial court in this case were based on reasonable inferences from the record, its findings must stand.

Gertz v. Bass (1965)

Facts: Gertz sued Bass for wrongful death and personal injuries resulting from a car crash. Without the knowledge of the court or either counsel, the bailiff gave the jury a dictionary during deliberations. This was an error because the dictionary had not been admitted into evidence and contained improper definitions of important legal terms. There was no way of knowing what actual use was made of the dictionary.

Issue: When is an error grounds for reversal?

Rule: An error is grounds for reversal only if it is prejudicial to the complaining party. However, in a situation where error is clear, the danger of prejudice is great, and proof of actual prejudice is difficult, prejudice may be inferred. Such is the case where a jury receives incompetent evidence; it is not necessary to prove that the jury gave the evidence any weight.

Bankers Trust Co. v. Mallis (S.Ct. 1978)

Facts: A district court dismissed a suit brought under the Securities Exchange Act of 1934, but did not enter judgment on a separate document. FRCP 58 stated that judgments are not effective unless set forth on a separate document. A final judgment is required for § 1291 appellate jurisdiction.

Issue: Can a district court decision be a final decision for purposes of § 1291 appellate jurisdiction if it is not set forth on a separate document?

Rule: (Per Curiam) The sole purpose of the separate document requirement is to clarify when the *time* for appeal begins to run. It is not a requirement for appellate *jurisdiction*. Thus, parties may waive the separate document requirement where a final judgment has been rendered but a separate document has accidentally not been entered.

FirsTier Mortgage Co. v. Investors Mortgage
Ins. Co. (S.Ct. 1991)

Facts: A judge announced that he intended to grant summary judgment, but he had yet to receive proposed findings of fact and conclusions of law, and he did not explicitly exclude the possibility that he would not change his mind before entering a final judgment. Following this announcement, but before judgment was entered, FirsTier filed a notice of appeal. FRAP 4(a)(2) permits notice of appeal to be filed "after the announcement of a decision or order."

Issue: Is notice of appeal premature where a court has announced that it intends to grant a final judgment, but has not yet terminated the litigation?

Rule: (Marshall, J.) FRAP 4(a)(2) permits notice of appeal following a nonfinal decision if the decision is of the type that would be appealable if immediately followed by the entry of judgment.

Chapter 11

RESPECT FOR JUDGEMENTS

I. INTRODUCTION

Preclusion of claims and issues is a long-standing tradition of Anglo-American jurisprudence. Litigants get one opportunity to litigate their case, and if they are unsuccessful, preclusion prevents relitigation even if the first trial did not achieve the optimally just result.

A. Policies
The idea that a judgment once made is binding on all future adjudications is rooted in several policies, including:

1. Avoidance of multiple suits on identical issues.

2. Reduction of all factually and legally related matters to single litigation.

3. Achievement of repose for the litigants.

4. Conservation of judicial resources.

5. Conservation of the litigants' resources.

6. Insurance of uniform application of the law.

B. Stare Decisis
This doctrine is not technically one of preclusion, since neither the same claims nor litigants are involved, generally, but many of the same policy considerations hold true. Under stare decisis, courts are bound by prior decisions of law made by superior courts, which will only overturn those decisions in cases of extreme prejudice or injustice.

II.   CLAIM PRECLUSION (RES JUDICATA)

After a valid and final judgment, a transactionally related claim may not be relitigated between the parties of the original suit.

A.   Same Claim

1. Transactional Test
The claim to be litigated may not involve the same transaction or occurrence, or series of transactions or occurrences, as a claim litigated in a prior suit.

2. One may not "sue hand by hand or finger by finger."
For instance, a driver damaged in a car accident could not bring separate suits for damage to the driver's legs, the driver's back, the neck, etc. These are clearly transactionally related. However damage to an auto and to the driver in one accident would not be transactionally related. Similarly, if the other driver slandered the plaintiff several days later by referring to the plaintiff's poor driving abilities, that would not be transactionally related to the claims of physical injury.

B.   Same Parties

1. Generally
Parties are bound by a prior decision only when those present in the second suit, or those in privity with the parties, were present in the first suit.

2. Privity
Parties who represent others or are contractually bound to accept liabilities at issue on the case are considered to have been present at the original suit for purposes of claim preclusion. Typical examples of privity include:

a. Representatives
Trustees, guardians, executors, agents, etc.

b. Class Action Representatives
One of the benefits of a class action is that the claims of many plaintiffs are resolved in one action. To allow class members to relitigate their claims would disembowel the efficacy of the class action.

c. Coparties Adjudicating a Finite Resource
For claim preclusion to apply, the parties must generally have been adverse to each other in the original suit. The exception to this rule occurs with adjudications of finite resources (water rights, in rem action, etc.). There, although the parties may nominally be on the same side of the litigation, since everybody's share depends on the legal rights of the others, everybody is essentially adverse to each other.

d. Nonparties
In *Nevada v. United States,* parties not present in the original suit were bound under claim preclusion. However, that case was special in that it involved water rights upon which many people had relied to their detriment.

e. Laboring Oar
A party not technically present in the original suit may be bound by claim preclusion if they had been so involved in directing the first suit that they could be said to have had a "laboring oar" in the conduct of the litigation. *Montana v. United States.*

3. Parties have no duty to join a lawsuit, and if not joined, they will generally not be bound by claim preclusion.

C. Valid and Final Judgment

1. Validity
A judgment is valid unless procured through fraud or corruption, or where there was a lack of personal or

subject matter jurisdiction, or there had been no opportunity to be heard.

2. Finality

a. Decision on the Merits
Defining a final judgment is no easy task. Generally, any decision on the merits of the case is final.

b. FRCP 12(b)(1)-(5),(7)
Dismissals due to lack of subject matter jurisdiction, lack of personal jurisdiction, improper venue, or insufficient process or service of process, or failure to join an indispensable party (FRCP 12(b)) are not final judgments.

c. FRCP 12(b)(6)
Dismissal for failure to state a claim upon which relief may be granted is a final judgment unless expressly dismissed without prejudice.

d. Unappealed Judgments
Decisions that could have been appealed, but were not, are final judgments.

e. Ripeness
Dismissal because a claim is not sufficiently ripe (see Justiciability) is not a final judgment.

D.   Counterclaims

1. Permissive Counterclaims
Permissive counterclaims are generally not precluded from future litigation, because they are generally not transactionally related to the case at hand.

2. Compulsory Counterclaims
By definition, compulsory counterclaims must be brought in the original suit or be barred from future litigation.

Compulsory counterclaims are generally transactionally related to the case at hand. An exception exists where the court deciding the first suit decided in favor of the defendant but cannot afford that party full relief on the counterclaim.

III.   ISSUE PRECLUSION (COLLATERAL ESTOPPEL)

When an issue of fact or law is **actually litigated** and determined by a **valid and final judgment**, and the determination is **essential to the judgment**, the determination is conclusive in a subsequent action between the **parties**, whether on the same or a different claim. *Restatement (Second) Judgments* § 27

A.   Actually Litigated

1. Similar Facts
   Similar facts do not mean that the issue was actually litigated. In *Cromwell v. County of Sac*, the court held that a finding of fraud in the conveyance of one coupon of interest was not preclusive for other coupons of interest, even though the coupons all came from the same municipal bond.

2. Burdens of Proof
   An issue may not have been actually litigated if the first issue had a lower burden of proof. For instance, just because a defendant was held to have committed assault in a civil case (preponderance of the evidence), does not mandate a finding of assault in a criminal case (beyond a reasonable doubt).

   Likewise, a verdict of not guilty on a criminal assault charge does not preclude a finding of assault in a civil tort case, where the plaintiff's burden is much lower.

B.   Essential to the Judgment
It must be shown that the issue alleged to have preclusive effect had to be decided by the decisionmaker at the first trial.

    1. Multiple Theories
Where a decision could have been rendered on any of several theories, without a special verdict no facts may turn out to have subsequent preclusive effect.

    2. Proximate v. Ultimate Facts
In *The Evergreens v. Nunan,* Judge Hand noted that not all trivial facts should be given preclusive effect, even if they did turn out to be essential to the judgment. Although he tried to distinguish between proximate facts (no preclusion) that were mere intermediary steps and ultimate facts (preclusion), the distinction remains hazy. Some factors that could be helpful in such an analysis is whether the parties actively litigated the issue, whether the issue is "trivial," or whether the importance of the fact could have been foreseen.

C.   Same Parties

    1. Traditional Rule — Mutuality
As in claim preclusion, the traditional rule had been that in order to assert issue preclusion the same parties or their privies had to have been present at the original case. The general rule was that if you could not estop your adversary, they could not estop you.

    2. Modern Rule — Nonmutuality
The doctrine of mutuality given way to a more flexible standard of nonmutual collateral estoppel. Not all jurisdictions recognize nonmutual collateral estoppel, and some only recognize defensive nonmutual collateral estoppel.

a. Defensive Nonmutual Collateral Estoppel
Where a plaintiff had already received an adverse judgment on an issue, a defendant not party or privy to that first suit could use that judgment to estop the plaintiff from subsequently relitigating that claim.

b. Offensive Nonmutual Collateral Estoppel
Where a defendant has already litigated an issue and lost, a plaintiff not party to the first suit may use that judgment to estop the defendant from asserting the same defense.

c. Mutuality and the United States as a Party
Because there is only one government, requiring the United States to be bound by the first decision on an issue could result in severe public costs. Furthermore, given the limited resources of the government, the Supreme Court has been reluctant to extend the principles of nonmutual collateral estoppel against the government.

   i. Defensive Collateral Estoppel
   The government may assert defensive nonmutual collateral estoppel when sued, as any private litigant.

   ii. Offensive Collateral Estoppel
   In *United States v. Mendoza*, the Court refused to allow a private party to assert offensive nonmutual collateral estoppel against the government. However, mutual collateral estoppel is still available. *United States v. Stauffer Chemical Company*. It would be unfair to let the United States use its resources to get favorable legal rulings by bankrupting a single defendant through legal fees.

D. Valid and Final Judgment
The standard here is generally identical as that for claim preclusion, above.

E.   Exceptions (*Restatement (Second) Judgments § 28*)

1. Party to be precluded could not by law have obtained review of the judgment in the first action.

2. There has been an intervening change in the applicable law.

3. To enforce the collateral estoppel would result in an inequitable administration of law.

4. The second court has very different procedures or rules, warranting relitigation.

5. The party to be precluded had to meet a heavier burden of persuasion in the first suit, the burden is on another party, or the party requesting preclusion has a heavier burden in the second suit.

6. The public interest warrants relitigation.

7. The effects of the preclusion were not foreseeable at the time the first action was litigated.

8. The party to be precluded did not have a full and fair opportunity to litigate the issues.

IV.   INTERSYSTEM PRECLUSION

A.   Interstate Preclusion

1. The Full Faith and Credit Clause
The Constitution, Art. IV, § 1, stipulates that every court in the nation must accord "full faith and credit" to the prior decisions of other courts in the country.

2. Full Faith and Credit Act (28 U.S.C. § 1738)
   Enacted pursuant to the Full Faith and Credit Clause, this statute clarifies what constitutes a valid decision, and what deference it is entitled in the courts.

3. Effect
   A decision of a sister state is given as much deference as it would receive in the state issued, even if not enforceable in the forum state.

4. Child Custody (28 U.S.C. § 1738A)
   Even though child custody orders are not technically "final" because the issuing court generally reserves the right to modify the order to protect the needs of the child, this act prevents other courts from modifying such orders unless:

   a. The state is the home state of the child;

   b. No other state would have jurisdiction;

   c. The child was abandoned in the state, or some other emergency exists; or

   d. The state that originally issued the order has declined jurisdiction.

B. Preclusive Effect of State Judgments in Federal Courts
   Although the Full Faith and Credit Clause only applies to the states, the Full Faith and Credit Statute (28 U.S.C. § 1738) extends the same requirements to the federal courts as well.

C. Preclusive Effect of Federal Judgments in State Courts
   Although statutory and constitutional authority is murky, most observers agree that states must afford federal judgments the same full faith and credit as afforded to decisions of sister states. This rule has never been seriously challenged.

D.   Preclusive Effect of Foreign Judgments
    Absent a treaty, judgments of foreign nations are not given
    full faith and credit. However, the United States has such
    treaties with most countries.

CASE CLIPS

Frier v. City of Vandalia (1985)

Facts: Vandalia towed four of Frier's cars because they were
blocking traffic. He brought an action for replevin in Illinois state
court and lost, the court having determined that the City had the
right to tow the cars. Frier then brought an action in federal court,
alleging violation of his Fourteenth Amendment Due Process rights
and 42 U.S.C. § 1983.
Issue: Does claim preclusion bar a suit that is based on the same
facts as a prior suit, but propounds a different legal theory?
Rule: A suit is barred by claim preclusion if it arises out of the
same core of operative facts or the same transaction that gave rise
to the original suit, even if the first suit was decided on different
grounds than those advanced in the second suit.
Concurrence: In determining whether disposition of a claim in
state court precludes a subsequent claim in federal court, the
federal court should apply the state's res judicata law. Here,
Illinois adheres to the traditional "common core of operative facts"
standard. The court should not apply the more expansive "transaction" test.

Martino v. McDonald's System, Inc. (1979)

Facts: McDonald's sued Martino because Martino breached a
provision in their franchise agreement that provided he would not
acquire a financial interest in a competing self-service food
business. The suit was terminated in favor of McDonald's by a
consent judgment (on the merits) before an answer was filed.
Martino brought the present action, alleging that enforcement of
the franchise restriction violated the Sherman Act. McDonald's
asserted that the new action was barred by FRCP 13(a), which

provided that a *pleading* must state as a counterclaim any claim the *pleader* has against the opposing party arising out of the same transaction. McDonald's also asserted that the suit was barred by common law principles of res judicata.

Issue 1:   When does FRCP 13(a) bar a claim arising out of a transaction that was the subject of a prior suit?

Rule 1:   FRCP 13(a) bars claims that are not raised during p-leading. It does not bar claims asserted by one who filed no pleadings in a prior suit. Because Martino's first action was terminated before he filed an answer, FRCP 13(a) does not bar him from bringing a claim arising out of the same transaction.

Issue 2:   Does res judicata bar a claim that arose out of a transaction that was the subject of a prior suit, but was not litigated in the prior suit?

Rule 2:   Res judicata treats a judgment on the merits as an absolute bar to relitigation between the parties of every matter that was offered or could have been offered to sustain or defeat a prior claim. Similarly, precedent and policy require that res judicata bar a counterclaim when its prosecution would nullify rights established by a prior action. Martino's antitrust claim would have been an appropriate defense in his first suit, and its successful prosecution might have nullified rights established in the prior action. Thus, Martino was not permitted to bring the antitrust claim in a second action.

Searle Bros. v. Searle (1978)

Facts: In a divorce suit, a court determined that the Slaugh House property was part of the marital property and awarded it all to Mrs. Searle. Searle Brothers, a partnership comprised of Searle's sons, brought this action to claim that they had a one-half interest in the property, having purchased it with partnership funds. The trial court ruled that their claim was precluded, even though they were not parties to the original action.

Issue: May collateral estoppel be applied against a party who was not a party to the original action?

Rule: Because a party is only subject to judgments or decrees of courts if their interests were legally represented, collateral estoppel can only be asserted against a party in a subsequent suit who was a party or in privity with a party in the prior suit. A person is in privity with another if their interests are so closely identified that they represent the same legal right. Collateral estoppel was not properly applied to Searle Brothers because it was not a party to the first suit and there was not sufficient evidence to show that its interest in the property was ever litigated.

Saylor v. Lindsley (1972)

Facts: Saylor, a class representative in a shareholder derivative action, appealed the settlement made by his attorney. Saylor had neither known of any settlement negotiation nor approved of the settlement offer. Saylor's attorney had engaged in little discovery before accepting settlement.

Issue: May an attorney representing a plaintiff in a class action derivative suit settle the case without approval of the plaintiff-representative?

Rule: An attorney must keep his client informed of settlement negotiations, advise the client before signing a stipulation of settlement on his behalf, and inform the court of any objections made by the client so that it can devise procedures to allow the plaintiff to conduct further inquiry. Furthermore, settlement in a class action shareholder derivative suit by the plaintiff's attorney should not be approved over plaintiff's opposition when doubt exists as to whether there has been a truly adversary discovery prior to the stipulation of settlement.

Illinois Central Gulf R.R. v. Parks (1979)

Facts: Mr. & Mrs. Parks brought a suit against Illinois Central following a collision between their car and a train. Mrs. Parks successfully sought damages for personal injuries. Mr. Parks unsuccessfully sought damages for loss of Mrs. Parks' services, consortium, etc. Thereafter, he brought a second suit seeking damages for his own personal injuries. Illinois Central argued that the new action was bared by claim preclusion,

Issue: When does estoppel by judgment (claim preclusion) apply?

Rule: Estoppel by judgment precludes the relitigation of a cause of action finally determined between two parties, and decrees that a judgment rendered is a complete bar to any subsequent action on the *same* claim or cause of action. Here, the court held that Mr. Parks could proceed with his suit because his claim for personal injuries required adjudication of certain issues, such as contributory negligence, that were not necessarily resolved in conjunction with his claim for loss of consortium.

Halpern v. Schwartz (1970)

Facts: A court found that Halpern committed "an act of bankruptcy" after a creditor alleged that she had committed three such acts, one of which was transferring property with the intent to hinder, delay or defraud. Any or all of them would have been grounds for the court's finding. A creditor brought a second action to prevent Halpern from receiving a bankruptcy discharge, also on the grounds that she transferred property with the intent to hinder, defraud or delay.

Issue: When a prior judgment is based on more than one independent, alternative ground, is a party precluded from relitigating any of those grounds?

Rule: Although an issue may have been fully litigated in a prior action, the prior judgment will not preclude reconsideration of the same issue if that issue did not necessarily determine the prior judgment. This is because an issue that was not essential to the prior judgment may not have been subject to the careful deliberation and analysis normally applied to essential issues, since a different disposition would not have affected the judgment. Also, a decision on an inessential issue is not subject to the safeguard of appellate review.

Winters v. Lavine (1978)

Facts: Winters was denied Medicaid compensation for Christian Science treatment. She brought a claim in state court, which was denied because 1) the statute that denied her claim was constitutional; or 2) she did not present sufficient proof of illness and treatment. She brought a second suit in federal court, alleging that the statute violated her constitutional rights.

Issue: When a prior judgment is based on more than one independent, alternative ground, is a party precluded from relitigating all of those grounds?

Rule: A party is barred from litigating any alternative grounds that were litigated in a prior action, so long as the plaintiff could fully anticipate the potential barring effect of the earlier judgment.

Such is the situation in the instant case, where both grounds were fully briefed and discussed at length in the first court's decision.

Parklane Hosiery Co. v. Shore
(S.Ct. 1979)

Facts: Shore brought a stockholder's class action against Parklane Hosiery for damages caused by a materially false and misleading proxy statement. Before this action came to trial in state court, the SEC filed suit against Parklane Hosiery in federal district court, alleging the same violations, and won. SEC actions do not receive jury consideration. Shore moved for partial summary judgment on the issues that had been resolved in the SEC action.

Issue: Can one who was not a party to the first suit offensively assert collateral estoppel to prevent a party from relitigating issues resolved in the first suit?

Rule: (Stewart, J.) A litigant who was not a party to a prior judgment may use that judgment offensively to prevent a party from relitigating issues resolved in an earlier suit.

Dissent: (Rehnquist, J.) The Seventh Amendment requires that in order to estop a claim, it must first have been litigated before a forum where a jury trial is available.

State Farm Fire & Cas. Co. v. Century Home Components
(1976)

Facts: A fire started in Century Home Components' ["Century"] shed and damaged many nearby properties. Century won the first two actions that reached judgment, but it was found negligent in the third. State Farm sought to use the third judgment to collaterally estop Century Home from denying liability in the instant action.

Issue: Can issue preclusion apply if prior suits have reached inconsistent verdicts regarding the issue in question?

Rule: Where there have been several lawsuits with varying verdicts, issue preclusion will not apply, even if the identical-issue and fully-and-fairly-litigated requirements are satisfied.

Federated Department Stores v. Moitie (S.Ct. 1981)

Facts: Moitie and others all lost in separate suits against the Federated Department Stores. The other independent plaintiffs gained reversal on appeal. Without appealing, Moitie brought the present action, alleging the same injury and facts. The Federated Department Stores asserted res judicata.

Issue: Does res judicata bar relitigation of an unappealed adverse judgment when other plaintiffs in similar suits against the same defendants successfully appealed the judgments?

Rule: (Rehnquist, J.) Res judicata bars the relitigation of an unappealed adverse judgment, even though other plaintiffs in similar suits against common defendants successfully appealed the judgments against them.

Concurrence: (Blackmun, J.) Sometimes, but not here, the doctrine of res judicata must give way to "overriding concerns of public policy and simple justice." Second, res judicata applies not only to those claims that were actually litigated, but to all claims that could have been litigated.

United States v. Mendoza (S.Ct. 1984)

Facts: The Nationality Act provided that noncitizens who served honorably with the United States during World War II were exempt from some nationality requirements. Due to political pressure, however, the Attorney General revoked the authority of the Immigration and Naturalization Service to grant these exemptions. In the first suit, sixty-eight Filipino war veterans challenged the Attorney General's action and prevailed. In the second suit, Mendoza, a Filipino war veteran not included in the first claim, asserted the same claim as the previous sixty-eight veterans.

Issue: May a plaintiff suing the United States use a prior case to which the plaintiff was not a party to preclude the government from asserting the same defense asserted in the first suit?

Rule: (Rehnquist, J.) A private party may not assert offensive nonmutual collateral estoppel against the United States Government.

Durfee v. Duke (S.Ct. 1963)

Facts: Durfee brought a suit in Nebraska state court to quiet title to land beneath the Missouri river. There was a question of fact as to whether the land was in Nebraska or Missouri. If the land was in Missouri, Nebraska would not have subject matter jurisdiction. The Nebraska court determined that the land was in Nebraska.

Two months later, Duke filed a suit to quiet title in Missouri state court, which was subsequently removed to federal court on the basis of diversity. An appellate court held that the district court did not need to give full faith and credit to the Nebraska judgment.

Issue: Must courts give full faith and credit to decisions rendered in other jurisdictions?

Rule: (Stewart, J.) Full faith and credit requires every state to give a judgment at least the res judicata effect that the judgment would be accorded in the state that rendered it. This even applies to challenges to the other court's jurisdiction, so long as the question was fully and fairly litigated and finally decided in the court that rendered the original judgment. Thus, the District Court must enforce the Nebraska judgment because Nebraska would enforce the Nebraska judgment.

Rozier v. Ford Motor Co. (1978)

Facts: Mr. Rozier was killed because the gas tank of his Ford exploded when struck from behind. In a wrongful death action brought by Mrs. Rozier, Ford was served with an interrogatory requesting any cost/benefit analyses about gas tank designs. Ford replied that it had no such information. They found the information shortly before trial, but they never disclosed it. Mrs. Rozier moved for a new trial on grounds of fraud, pursuant to FRCP-60(b)(3).

Issue: Is it proper to grant a new trial after judgment because of party's misconduct?

Rule: A party is entitled to a new trial upon proof that misrepresentation and other misconduct by their adversary prevented them from fully and fairly presenting their case.

Table of Authorities

Table of Cases

BLOND'S™
LAW GUIDES